D1082100

THE RATHBONE YEARS

Masterpieces acquired for the
Museum of Fine Arts, Boston, 1955–1972
and for the
St. Louis Art Museum, 1940–1955

THE RATHBONE YEARS

*Masterpieces acquired for the
Museum of Fine Arts, Boston, 1955-1972
and for the
St. Louis Art Museum, 1940-1955*

Museum of Fine Arts, Boston   1972

All Rights Reserved

by Museum of Fine Arts, Boston, Massachusetts

Library of Congress catalog card no. 72-81916

ISBN 0-87846-067-5

Printed in Germany by Brüder Hartmann, West Berlin

Designed by Carl F. Zahn

CONTENTS

FOREWORD

It is a fine, well-established custom to honor a retiring director of an art museum with an exhibition of his outstanding acquisitions. "By their fruits ye shall know them." The curatorial staff of the Boston Museum enthusiastically followed the tradition. This show and its accompanying catalog represent a work of love, a tribute to Perry Rathbone.

The selection, in which each art department is equally represented in quality, if not in quantity, is determined chiefly by the works that are especially dear to Perry Rathbone, and with whose acquisition he was especially involved, but also by the number of special exhibition galleries at our disposal. It proved to be impossible to accommodate in this limited space all the objects each department wished to display; those that could not be included in this exhibit may be found in the permanent galleries, with red stickers on their labels marking them as acquisitions of the Rathbone years.

For many the exhibition will be a surprise, because it is not exclusively an exhibition of pictures. Strange as it may seem, for a great part of the general public art is still identified solely with painting, and a museum director's fame is measured by the acquisition of paintings by internationally established masters. Certainly, Perry Rathbone added to the collection such great names as Lucas van Leyden, Rosso Fiorentino, Rembrandt, Tiepolo, Manet, Degas, and Picasso! But he also added the great Flemish triptych of the Martyrdom of St. Hippolytus, *a work completely unknown at the time of its sale, and one that even museums of much greater means had not the courage to purchase, for it could not be attributed to a known artist. Further study might well identify it as a work of Hugo van der Goes; but even if he is not known, the "Master of the Boston Martyrdom of St. Hippolytus" will always be one of the outstanding artistic personalities in fifteenth-century Flemish painting. The supplementing of all these great works with related choice examples by the so-called demigods, the* petits maîtres—*not for the sake of art-historical, encyclopedic completion but for the purpose of harmony and unity of aesthetic experience—is no small achievement of Perry Rathbone's collecting policy.*

Artistic interaction and balanced integration are expressed here not only in paintings but also in works of art of widely divergent nature: prints and drawings, textiles, metalwork, ceramics, and sculpture. The arts of the Far and Near East, of Egypt, Greece, and Italy, northern Europe and America can be experienced in resplendent radiation.

George H. Edgell, Perry Rathbone's predecessor, once said "If an indiscreet museum director were asked point blank what aspect of his work he was proudest of, he would probably reply that it was the quality of the acquisitions made by the museum during his regime. Of course, no one individual makes the acquisitions. They are made on the recommendation of a curator, fortified by the

7

recommendation of the director, and decided by the trustees or a committee thereof. Nevertheless, an honest director would admit that he regards acquisitions made during his directorship as his." Inspired by and inspiring curators, Perry Rathbone became with his staff, in a manner of speaking, a creative collective personality.

A tribute to Perry Rathbone, this exhibition will, we hope, serve also as a lesson for the future in pointing out qualities and requirements essential, in our view, to a creative and successful museum director. These are, first and foremost, consecration to art throughout life and training by and association with those who are able to convey their dedication, knowledge, and experience to the neophyte in the profession. Paul J. Sachs at Harvard, W. R. Valentiner at the Detroit Museum, and Curt Valentin in New York were Perry Rathbone's counselors and friends. A buoyant enthusiasm and insatiable appetite for pure artistic creation, not prejudiced or inhibited by historical specialization, always motivated his response to beauty and his collecting policy. His never-tiring eye immediately perceived the gaps in various fields, and he tried to fill them whenever an opportunity was offered, always avoiding the danger of accepting merely "art historical" objects. An unfaltering belief in the ennobling and refining influence of art on the human spirit protected his consistency of vision from the demands and pressures made upon a museum director.

For Perry Rathbone art remains central to everything. I vividly recall that, at a tense moment between meetings on the museum's centennial program and on the financial situation, I showed Perry photographs of our knightly saddle (no. 54), which had unexpectedly appeared on the market. It was without doubt the worst moment to plead for the acquisition of this unique object, and yet he did not fail to show excitement and encouragement. My fellow curators could speak of similar experiences. They knew they could make the director change his itinerary abroad, no matter how tight the schedule, in order to see and to judge an object offered for purchase. Perry Rathbone firmly believes that without intensification of its acquisition program, not in a quantitative but in a qualitative way, an art museum would lose its raison d'être.

To illustrate the growing consistency of Perry Rathbone's artistic vision, a selection of his purchases for the St. Louis Art Museum, of which he was director before coming to Boston, is included in this exhibition*. For the same reason it was also planned to include a selection from his private collection. We regret that this could not be realized for the moment. This selection would have given fascinating evidence of his early interest in Americana, primitive art, ceramics, modern prints and drawings, sculpture and painting, long before they became fashionable. An American primitive portrait hung over the mantlepiece in his college room. He acquired works by Lee Gatch and David Smith, by Kirchner, Nolde, and Klee before he became a museum director. His portrait by Max Beckmann (frontispiece), painted in 1948, a year after the artist's appointment to Washington University, St. Louis (an appointment for which Perry Rathbone was chiefly responsible), is the only example representing his private collection.

---

* For this section of the catalogue Mr. Rathbone kindly agreed to contribute a perface, (see p. 189).

8

The same spirit, the same consistency of vision, never pedantically categorical or programmatic, informed his personality—a personality full of natural warmth and enthusiasm. It is this trait that brought forth friends and benefactors to the museum. Space prevents stretching out a catalogue of indebtedness, but it would be inexcusable not to mention here Forsyth Wickes, R. Thornton Wilson, John Goelet, and the family of the late Governor Alvan T. Fuller.

With all his flair for attracting attention to galleries badly in need of renovation, not to mention whole departments in similar need, and with his ability to create special exhibitions, he was never tempted by overdramatic effects or led by dictates of fashion; he was led solely by the ideal of strengthening artistic content and experience. Up to the final moment before an opening, last refinements of spacing and lighting were tried. The principle was never to impair the state of harmonious intimacy and contemplation required for the enjoyment and under-standing of art.

Again, it would take too much space to list all the transformations and all the special exhibitions of the Rathbone years. Our memories are short, and many may have forgotten the deeds. Hence, a prominent space in the show goes to the dis-play of special exhibition catalogues, as well as publications on the permanent collection, that were initiated and encouraged by Perry Rathbone. The list is impressive indeed. I should like to single out European Masters of Our Time *(1957),* Masterpieces of Primitive Art *(1958),* Art of Ancient Peru *(1961),* Gold of Ancient America *(1968), in order to record Perry Rathbone's whole-hearted in-volvement in contemporary, Pre-Columbian, and primitive art, years before independent departments for these fields were established.*

Not included in this show are Perry Rathbone's contributions in the museum's annual reports from 1955 to 1971. But I should like to recommend them as re-quired reading to those concerned with the functions and needs of art museums. They will offer a younger generation of museum directors valuable thought and inspiration as, I trust, exhibition also does.

Hanns Swarzenski

I ANCIENT ART

1

Cycladic idol

Third millennium B.C.; Central Aegean island marble; h. 1.11 m.
Gift of Miss Alice Tully and Centennial Purchase Fund. 67.758

*The idol is larger than nearly every other example surviving from antiquity. The rich
yellow patina is made up of incrustation tempered by areas of surface pitting. Broken,
in antiquity, at the neck and just below the knees, the idol was probably deliberately
separated into three pieces to fit into a small tomb that could not have held a sculpture of this size. Her fingers, toes, and backbone are incised. There are faint traces of her
eyes. She is the absolute expression of Greek monumental sculpture in marble nearly
fifteen hundred years before the beginnings of Archaic Greek art.*

References: *Centennial Acquisitions*, special issue of *Boston Museum Bulletin* 68 (1970), 14–15,
no. 1; D. Pickman, *Archaeology*, April 1970, cover illus; C. Vermeule, *Burlington Magazine*,
January 1971, 37–38, fig. 46.

2

Fragment of limestone vessel

Sumerian, Protoliterate period, ca. 3200 B.C.; limestone; h. 16 cm., w. 22 cm.
William Francis Warden Fund. 63.1258

*The importance of the herds in the temple economy of early Sumer is emphasized in its
art, particularly in a series of ritual vessel in stone with friezes of cattle, goats, and sheep
modeled with the heads turned toward the viewer. In the Boston vessel the bulls are
strongly modeled in high relief with the parts clearly articulated through three-dimen-
sionality and incised lines.*

Reference: Edward L. B. Terrace, "Recent Acquisitions in the Department of Egyptian Art,"
Museum of Fine Arts, Boston, *Bulletin* 62 (1964), 55–56, fig. 9.

3

Fragment of a victory stela

Mesopotamia, Dynasty of Akkad, probably reign of Naram-Sin, ca. 2230–2194 B.C.; alabaster; h. 35 cm., w. 11.5 cm.

Gift of the Guide Foundation through Dr. and Mrs. Edmundo Lassalle. 66.893

The theme of enemy prisoners brought by officers and soldiers before the conqueror is one of the oldest and longest lasting in the representational arts of the Ancient Near East. The Boston fragment of an Akkadian stela exhibits a gemlike workmanship in its treatment of the helmeted and bearded warrior following a file of bound captives. The arm of the preceding figure with ropes is preserved on the same fragment. In an adjoining fragment, now in the Baghdad Museum, the naked prisoners are shown with necks held in a wooden stock and arms bound behind them. Note the contrast between the subtly modeled face, arms, and torso and the minute details of the mustache, beard, and fingernail, as well as the fittings of the hafted axe.

References: Centennial Acquisitions, special issue of *Boston Museum Bulletin* 68 (1970), 15; John F. X. McKeon, "An Akkadian Victory Stele," *Boston Museum Bulletin* 68 (1970), 226–243, figs. 1–3, 6.

14

4

Votive double axe

Late Minoan I, ca. 1500 B.C.; gold; l. (of shaft) 0.09 m., w. 0.083 m.

Theodora Wilbour Fund in memory of Zoë Wilbour. 58.1009

The ceremonial double axe is inscribed with a very rare example of the Minoan script known as Linear A. A hoard of such axes, mostly in bronze and silver, was found in one of the sacred caves of Crete, at Arkalochori on Mount Dikte. These axes were considered as votives to the presiding goddess. A clue to the name of this goddess appears on the museum's example, where the inscription can be transliterated possibly as "To (?) Demeter" or "(Mount) Ida-Mother."

References: Emily T. Vermeule, "A Gold Minoan Double Axe," Museum of Fine Arts, Boston, *Bulletin* 57 (1959), 4–16, fig. 1, and cover; W. J. Young, "Technical Examination of a Minoan Gold Double Axe," ibid., 17–20, figs. 1–4; G. Chase and C. Vermeule, *Greek, Etruscan & Roman Art: The Classical Collection in the Museum of Fine Arts, Boston,* rev. ed. (Boston, 1963), pp. 14–15, 22, fig. 10.

5

Statuette of Amunhotpe III

Egypt, Dynasty 18, reign of Amunhotpe III, ca. 1400 B.C.; steatite with traces of glaze; h. 12.8 cm., w. of base 3.5 cm., l. of base 5.5 cm.

Gift of Mrs. Horace L. Mayer. 1970.636

The Mayer statuette of Amunhotpe III depicts the king kneeling to present a phylactery to the god. The features are more those of a prince than a king, and both face and body exhibit a youthful chubbiness that was to give way to the flabby corpulence shown in his later representations.

References: William Kelly Simpson, "A Statuette of Amunhotpe III in the Museum of Fine Arts, Boston," *Boston Museum Bulletin* 68 (1970), 260–269; *Sotheby Sale Catalogue,* 29 November 1965, no. 144 B; William Kelly Simpson, "Egyptian and Ancient Near Eeastern Art in Boston, 1970–71," *Burlington Magazine* 114 (1972), in press.

6

Fragment of column drum from Amarna

Egypt, Dynasty 18, reign of Akhenaten, 1363–1347 B.C.; limestone; h. 22 cm., circ. of arc 60 cm.

Edward J. and Mary S. Holmes Fund. 67.637

The extensive palaces and temples of the reign were constructed of small blocks in the manner of brickwork, an archaizing feature harking back perhaps to the earliest Egyptian architecture. When the buildings were dismantled by Akhenaten's successors, the thousands of blocks separated from their compositional context become like fragments in a puzzle, with heads and bodies rarely on the same block. The Boston section of a column drum shows the king on the right followed by Nefertiti, who holds a libation vessel aloft, and the princess Meritaten bearing a sistrum. Behind the latter is a representation of the same princess from a similar scene, facing in the opposite direction. Among the features of Amarna art represented are the long neck and exaggerated hips of the queen, the curiously shaped head of the princess, and the sun's rays ending in hands radiating from the right toward the royal family.

Reference: Edward L. B. Terrace, "The Age of Empire and Rebellion: The New Kingdom in Boston," *Connoisseur* 169 (1968), 54, fig 10.

7

Palace wine jar

Egypt, probably from Amarna, Dynasty 18, reign of Amunhotpe III or Akhenaten, 1402–1347 B.C.; pottery with light blue, black, and buff painted details; h. 74.5 cm. J. H. and E. A. Payne Fund. 64.9

The decorated pottery of the predynastic Egyptian cultures disappears with the advent of the dynastic period. Seldom does pottery again emerge as a vehicle for aesthetic expression. In the exuberant arts of the reigns of Amunhotpe III and Akhenaten vessels are painted in soft blue on a buff background with floral wreaths and plant and animal motives. They are probably inspired by the Aegean-influenced arts of the royal gold and copper smiths. The Boston amphora has a frieze of grapes below the rim. A gazelle sits on the shoulder with its feet tucked beneath it. On the lid is a seated heifer. The amphora is one of the finest of these palace vessels.

Reference: Edward L. B. Terrace, "Recent Acquisitions in the Department of Egyptian Art," Museum of Fine Arts, Boston, *Bulletin* 62 (1964), 48–52, figs. 1–3.

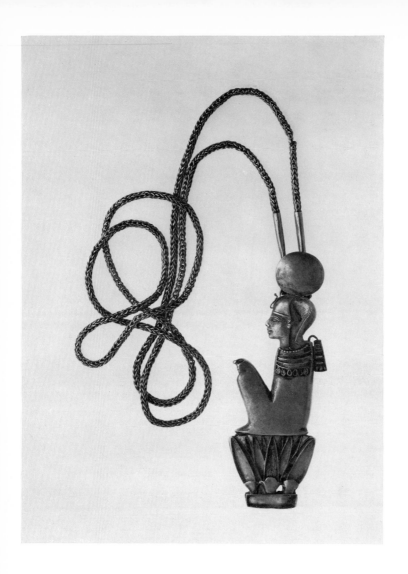

8

Pendant on chain

Egypt, Dynasty 19, probably reign of Ramses II, ca. 1285 B.C.; gold with traces of lapis and glass inlays; h. of pendant 7.2 cm., l. of chain 63 cm.

Gift of Mrs. Horace L. Mayer in memory of Horace L. Mayer. 68.836

The Mayer gold pendant represents the new-born sun god seated on an open lotus flower. Inlays of lapis and semiprecious stones or glass were set in the cloisons of the flower as well as in the hair lock and the necklace and its counterpoise. This extraordinary jewel, complete with its chain of interlocking gold links, may have come from the palace at Abu Gurob near the entrance to the Fayyum.

References: Cyril Aldred, *Jewels of the Pharoahs* (New York, 1971), p. 232, fig. 128; Edward L. B. Terrace, "The Age of Empire and Rebellion: The New Kingdom in Boston," *Connoisseur* 169 (1968), 49, figs. 1, 51, and cover; *Centennial Acquisitions*, special issue of *Boston Museum Bulletin* 68 (1970), 20–21.

9a *(see overleaf)*

Relief from palace of Sennacherib at Nineveh

Assyrian, reign of Sennacherib, 705–681 B.C.; limestone; h. 66 cm., L. 85 cm.

Charles Amos Cummings Bequest Fund and Gift of Horace L. Mayer. 60.133

Narrative art in the Assyrian palace reliefs was developed to illustrate the ritual activities of the kings and their widespread and recurrent military campaigns. These latter compositions, with their imposing sweep and topographical details, are best illustrated in the extensive series from several reigns that form part of the marvels brought to the British Museum by Sir Henry Austen Layard, an extraordinary man who numbered Disraeli among his friends. The two Boston reliefs are from the North Palace of Sennacherib at Nineveh. The first depicts the forced march of Babylonian women from their native palm groves to a distant exile. A mother is shown holding a leather water skin to her child. The latter steadies the skin with outstretched hands. In the second relief a soldier with shield and spear on the left climbs a mountainous region followed by an archer with his quiver. On the right an enemy soldier has apparently fallen from his horse while his companions hurl spears. One of them covers the archer with his shield to protect him from the Assyrian adversary.

References: Sotheby Sale Catalogue, 16 November 1959; William Stevenson Smith, "Two Assyrian Reliefs from Canford Manor," Museum of Fine Arts, Boston, *Bulletin* 58 (1960), 44–56, figs. 1–5; Edward L. B. Terrace, *The Art of the Ancient Near East in Boston* (Boston, 1962), nos. 23–24.

9b *(see overleaf)*

Relief from palace of Sennacherib at Nineveh

Assyrian, reign of Sennacherib, 705–681 B.C.; limestone; h. 84.5 cm., l. 64 cm.

Charles Amos Cummings Bequest Fund. 60.134

References: Sotheby Sale Catalogue, 16 November 1959; William Stevenson Smith, "Two Assyrian Reliefs fron Canford Manor," Museum of Fine Arts, Boston, *Bulletin* 58 (1960), 44–56, figs. 1–5; Edward L. B. Terrace, *The Art of the Ancient Near East in Boston* (Boston, 1962), nos. 23–24.

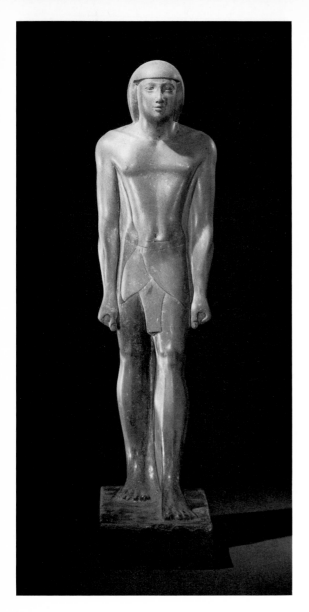

10

Standing statue attributed to the Vizier Bakenrenef
Egypt, Dynasty 26, reign of Psamtik I, 664–609 B.C.;
dark green schist; h. with restored feet and base
50 cm.
William E. Nickerson Fund No. 2 1970.495

The taut muscularity of the vizier's statue is miti-gated by a softness of the surface treatment. The face has an idealized cast, yet it lacks real indi-vidualization. The long arms convey a sense of straining muscles yet also impart a feeling of com-plete repose.

References: Collection *H. Hoffmann,* ed. G. Legrain
(Paris, 1894), no. 41, p. 16, pl. 9; William Kelly Simpson,
"Department of Egyptian and Ancient Near Eastern
Art," Museum of Fine Arts, Boston, *The Museum Year:*
1970–71 (Boston 1972), 44–45; idem, "Egyptian and An-
cient Near Eastern Art in Boston, 1970–71," *Burlington*
Magazine 114 (1972), in press; idem, "Three Egyptian
Statues of the Seventh and Sixth Centuries B.C."
Kemi 21 (1972), in press.

11

Headless block statue of Nesna-isut

Egypt, Dynasty 26, reign of Psamtik I, 664–609 B.C.; dark green schist; h. with base 37.5 cm., w. of base 16.2 cm., l. of base 31.3 cm.

Helen and Alice Colburn Fund. 68.152

Rarely does a block statue of the Late Period convey as much interest in the modeling of the body. With its head missing, the statue permits us to concentrate on the subtle relations of the parts and the surface treatment. Although the apron in front, with its inscription, and the belt indicate the presence of a garment, the sculptor has eliminated any trace of its lower edge on the sides. Even the knees and toes and the relation between the touching upper and lower leg are successfully expressed. The cartouches of the reigning king are inscribed on the arms, and two columns of text with the official's titles are inscribed on the back support.

Reference: B. Bothmer et al., *Egyptian Sculpture of the Late Period* (Brooklyn: The Brooklyn Museum, 1960), pp. 38–39, no. 32, pls. 30–31, figs. 68–70.

12

Circular cosmetic container

Anatolia, ca. Dynasty 26, 664–525 B.C.; green faience with details in blue; h. (with lid) 2.7 cm., diam. 6.3 cm.

Edward J. and Mary S. Holmes Fund. 1970.571

Said to have been found in Anatolia, the green faience box with four compartments may have been a wedding gift for a noble lady. Egypt exported luxury wares to the Mediterranean world at this time. The frog on the lid guards the contents with his legs alert and ready to spring. The bulging belly contrasts with the head and its fierce expression.

References: William Kelly Simpson, "Acquisitions in Egyptian and Ancient Near Eastern Art in the Boston Museum of Fine Arts, 1970–71," *Connoisseur* 179 (February 1972), 118–119, figs. 7, 7a.; idem, "Department of Egyptian and Ancient Near Eastern Art," Museum of Fine Arts, Boston, *The Museum Year: 1970–71* (Boston, 1972), 46.

13

Mountain sheep
Persia, Achaemenian, 6th-5th century B.C.; silver and gold-plated silver, hollow cast;
h. 4 cm., l. 7 cm.
J. H. and E. A. Payne Fund. 59.14

*There are few objects in the collection so appealing and irresistible as the little moun-
tain sheep, the head and horns of which were separately made and attached. Three of
the legs are three-dimensional, while the fourth, tucked underneath, is incised. Although certainly Achaemenian in origin, it was acquired from a dealer in Bombay.*

References: Edward L. B. Terrace, "Two Achaemenian Objects in the Boston Museum of Fine
Arts," *Antike Kunst* 6 (1963), 76–80, pl. 31, figs. 1–4; Museum of Fine Arts, Boston, *The Art of
the Ancient Near East in Boston* (Boston, 1962), no. 58; *Illustrated London News*, 8 September
1962, in color; Museum of Fine Arts, Boston, *Bulletin* 58 (1960), 42, fig. 15.

14

Stamp seal

Persia, Achaemenian, 5th century B.C.; chalcedony with gold mount; diam. 1.5 cm.
Gift of Mr. and Mrs. Donald P. Edgar. 66.1077

*Seals and coins often seem too small for major museum collections, but how false this
point of view is! Our visitors are invariably attracted to our collection of seals. This
light blue chalcedony seal shows two rearing affronted lions with their heads turned
back and roaring in suitable heraldic fashion. The feet are simply indicated by three
drilled dots. The fierceness of the lions is tamed by the placidity of the two duck heads
of the gold clasp.*

15

Bowl

Persia, Achaemenian, 5th century B.C.; silver with gold-plated overlays; hammer and punch worked, with chasing; h. 4 cm., diam. 19 cm.

Harriet Otis Cruft and Edwin E. Jack Funds. 60.535

Achaemenian plate shows a wide diversity in decoration, quality, and technique. The silver and gold-plated silver bowl in Boston is a masterwork of its type. A single piece of silver has been worked with hammer and punch and then chased in part to produce an exuberant yet strictly controlled twelve-section spider-web pattern, which ends in a frieze of alternating lotus flowers and palmettes. The central rosette boss and parts of the flowers and palmettes are overlaid with gold-plated silver.

References: Museum of Fine Arts, Boston, *Annual Report, 1960* (Boston, 1961), 50; Museum of Fine Arts, Boston, *The Art of the Ancient Near East in Boston* (Boston, 1962), no. 61, frontispiece in color; *Illustrated London News*, September 1962, color supplement; Edward L. B. Terrace, "Two Achaemenian Objects in the Boston Museum of Fine Arts," *Antike Kunst* 6 (1963), 72–76, pls. 29–30.

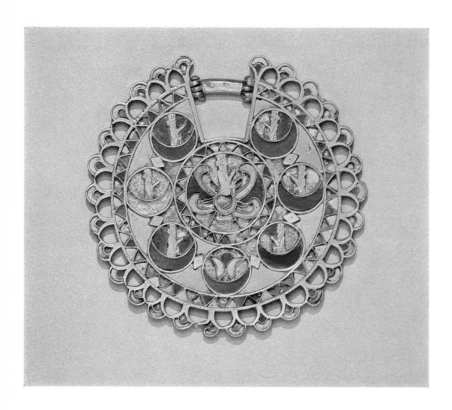

16

Earring

Western Asia, Achaemenian, 5th century B.C.; gold with inlays of lapis lazuli, turquoise, and carnelian; diam. 5 cm.

Edward J. and Mary S. Holmes Fund. 1971.256

The gaudy play of lapis, turquoise, carnelian, and gold makes this jewel a glorious achievement of the Achaemenian jeweler's art. The Boston earring, one of a pair found together, must have been its owner's pride. The figure of Ahura Mazda or the king is incised on a gold plaque seven times on each side and may have astronomical significance. Earrings of this shape and in similar cloison technique are known, but none surpass the brilliance and complexity of composition of our example.

References: William Kelly Simpson, "Acquisitions in Egyptian and Ancient Near Eastern Art in the Boston Museum of Fine Arts, 1970–71," *Connoisseur* 179 (February 1972), 119–120, fig. 8; "Treasures of Massachusetts," *Boston Globe*, 5 March 1972, special section, pp. 34–35.

30

17

Footed bowl

Persia, Sasanian, 6th century A.D.; silver with portions mercury gilded; diam. 21.2 cm.
J. H. and E. A. Payne Fund. 1971.52

A mountain sheep with trailing streamers, a favorite motif in Sasanian art, is shown
picking his way across flower-covered mountains toward a magical blossom. He wears a
bell attached to a studded collar and has a luxuriant fleece on his chest. The body, head,
horns, and blossom have been separately fashioned and applied to the surface as raised
relief. The sheep and the blossom have been mercury gilded.

References: Parke-Bernet Sales Catalogue, 28 January 1966, no. 147; William Kelly Simpson,
"Acquisitions in Egyptian and Ancient Near Eastern Art in the Boston Museum of Fine Arts,
1970–71," *Connoisseur* 179 (February 1972), 120, color plate on p. 115; idem, "Department of
Egyptian and Ancient Near Eastern Art," Museum of Fine Arts, Boston, *The Museum Year:*
1970–71 (Boston, 1972), 46.

18

Phrygian vessel with handle

Western Asia, ca. 625 B.C.; pottery with reddish brown painted scene and decoration;
h. 30 cm., diam. 25 cm.

Edward J. and Mary S. Holmes Fund. 1971.297

*Phrygian vase painting is nowhere better exemplified than in this oenochoe frieze of
the goddess Artemis-Cybele hunting a lion. The lively motion of the arrows in flight is
reminiscent of the lion hunt reliefs of Assurbanipal from Nineveh now in the British
Museum, which are a few decades earlier. A single line is effectively used to render
the profile and eye of the goddess. The claw like feet of the animals and the griffin with
bird head tail are features which reflect an ultimate North Syrian influence.*

Reference: William Kelly Simpson, "Century Two: Collecting Egyptian and Ancient Near Eastern
Art for the Boston Museum," *Apollo* 95 (1972), in press.

19 *(detail, p. 33)*
Attic black-figured amphora
Manner of Exekias; Archaic, ca. 540 B.C.; h. 0.52 m.
Henry Lillie Pierce Residuary Fund and Bartlett Collection. 63.952

On the principal side of the vase Dionysos is seated sipping wine from a kantharos as tiny satyrs frolic and shake grapes into baskets in a rich vineyard. On the other side, the Dioskouroi oversee the harnessing of a biga, or two-horse chariot, which Polydeukes is mounting. Helen stands at the left. Her younger brothers, the twins Kastor (in a long white robe) and Polydeukes, prepare their chariot for an outing in the countryside of Sparta. The heavenly pair were patrons of riders, sailors, and boxers.

References: Illustrated Handbook: Museum of Fine Arts, Boston, rev. ed. (Boston, 1964), pp. 50–51; G. M. A. Richter, *The Furniture of the Greeks, Etruscans, and Romans* (London, 1966), p. 44, fig. 240; M. Comstock and C. Vermeule, *Apollo,* December 1969, 469–470, fig. 4.

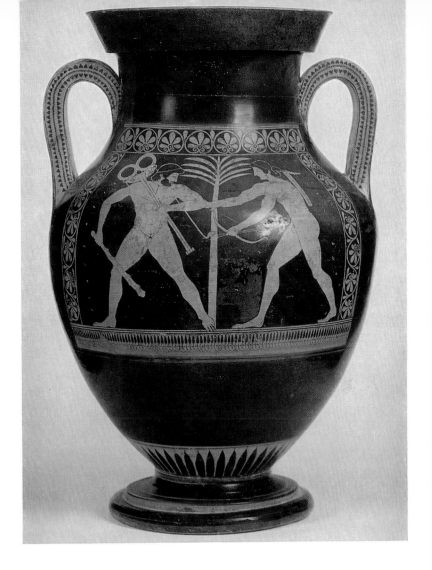

20

Attic red-figured amphora
Circle of Euthymides; ca. 510 B.C.; h. 0.65 m.
William Francis Warden, Catharine Page Perkins, and James Funds. 63.1515

On the principal side of this giant vase Herakles and Apollo struggle for the sacred tripod of Apollo's shrine at Delphi. Herakles has the tripod slung firmly across his right shoulder and holds his club in his lowered right hand. Apollo has seized Herakles by the left elbow and seems to threaten him with his bow. Intervention by the other Olympian divinities resulted in Herakles relinquishing the tripod, so necessary for the giving out of prophecies at the shrine on Mount Parnassus. On the second side of the vase, a maenad, follower of the wine god Dionysos, revels between two prancing, long-eared, horse-tailed Silens. This amphora is among the earliest monumental vases marking the full shift from black to red-figure as the method of decorative expression.

References: C. Vermeule, Museum of Fine Arts, Boston, *Bulletin* 61 (1963), 150 ff., figs. 1–2; W. M. Whitehill, *Museum of Fine Arts, Boston: A Centennial History* (Cambridge, Mass., 1970), vol. 2, p. 662, illus.; C. Vermeule, *Connoisseur*, May 1971, 38–39, 46–48, no. 15.

21

Head of a kouros, or youth
East Greek, 510–490 B.C.; Western Asia Minor marble; h. 0.27 m.
Centennial Gift of Landon T. Clay. 69.982

The unfinished head appears to have been part of a high relief. Such a monument must have been on a grand architectural scale, perhaps the lower section of a column or the altar of a temple. The face and hair were left as completed with a fine claw chisel, possibly during disturbances in the Graeco-Persian wars. The figure was presumably draped, like those found in abundance at the excavations of the Heraion on Samos. The youth could have been part of a procession of votaries or temple officials.

References: Boston Museum Bulletin 68 (1970), 22, no. 6, illus.; W. M. Whitehill, Museum of Fine Arts, Boston: A Centennial History (Cambridge, Mass., 1970), vol. 2, p. 658; C. Vermeule, Burlington Magazine, January 1971, 38, figs. 44–45.

22

Youth on horseback, with hound
Archaic, ca. 500 B.C.; terracotta; h. (to top of horseman's head) 0.60 m., l. (hound) 0.27 m.
William Francis Warden Fund. 65.463, 65.464

The ensemble, from Sicily, must have been produced around 500 B.C., for the face of the rider shows classic Greek Archaic characteristics, the bulging eyes and smile, while the the modeling of the horse's head seems more studied, more natural than is usual for horses before the beginning of the fifth century. There is no certain indication of how the hound was placed in relation to the horseman, although a slight depression on the plinth to the right rear of the horse suggests he could have been running there, close to the horse's hooves. The position of the petasos, or traveler's cap, has been determined by its size, the surfaces of the rider's head, and the interior of the cap.

References: C. Vermeule, *Boston Museum Bulletin* 64 (1966), 124–133, figs. 1–3; C. Vermeule, *Antike Plastik* 8 (1968), 7–11, figs. 1–2, pls. 1–4; W. M. Whitehill, *Museum of Fine Arts, Boston: A Centennial History* (Cambridge, Mass., 1970), vol. 2, pp. 659–660, illus.

23

Attic red-figured calyx-krater: The Fall of Troy

THE ALTAMURA PAINTER, 470–460 B.C.; h. 0.48 m., d. 0.49m.

William Francis Warden Fund. 59.178

Scenes from the Fall of Troy appear on both sides of the vase. King Priam, seated on an altar, watches Neoptolemos grasp Astyanax prior to hurling him from the walls. Cassandra clutches an image of Athena at the left while trying to save herself from Ajax. On the other side of the vase, Aeneas carries his father Anchises from the burning city. Creusa follows, and a young warrior, perhaps Ascanius, leads the way. The scenes were adapted from Homer and from lost epic poems dealing with the mythological war and its aftermath. A famous painting must have inspired the details, as the principal designs and motifs occur in certain scenes on other vases of the decades after 510 B.C. The krater's size has allowed the Altamura Painter to echo the monumentality of major compositions in his figures.

References: C. Vermeule, *Illustrated London News*, 10 October 1959, pp. 398–399, figs. 1–6; J. D. Beazley, *Attic Vase Painting in the Museum of Fine Arts, Boston* (Boston, 1963), vol. 3, pp. 61–65, no. 159, pls. 92–95, suppl. pls. 22–23; P. T. Rathbone, *Apollo*, January 1970, 57, fig. 3.

24

Funerary lion

Attic, ca. 390 B.C.; Pentelic marble; h. (at shoulder) 0.43 m., l. 1.22 m.

William Francis Warden Fund. 65.563

This Attic lion once graced the corner of a family lot in a cemetery near Athens. He had a companion of similar dimensions, facing in the opposite direction. African lions were hardly to be seen in Periklean Athens, and sculptors stuck to preconceived ideals of what a lion should be rather than to fidelities of nature. His teeth are bared in a snarl rather than a roar. The flamelike tufts and curls of the mane are arranged in rows in alternate directions. Careful restoration of the legs and tail was done by the museum's Research Laboratory.

References: C. Vermeule, *Classical Journal* 62 (1966), 106–107, fig. 15; C. Vermeule, *Boston Museum Bulletin* 65 (1967), 182, 184, fig. 8; W. M. Whitehill, *Museum of Fine Arts, Boston: A Centennial History* (Cambridge, Mass., 1970), vol. 2, pp. 656–657.

25

Head of Polyphemus
Hellenistic, 150–50 B.C.; Parian marble; h. 0.383 m.
Gift in honor of Edward W. Forbes from his friends. 63.120

*Cyclopean in size, the head comes from a colossal figure, perhaps part of a harbor group.
Polyphemus has been dated by competent scholars to about A.D. 100–110, but there is
nothing in the carving to suggest that the work is not as early as the second school of
Pergamon in the middle of the Hellenistic period. He is based, in details of hair and
beard, on a Pergamene centaur. The one-eyed Cyclops looks as savagely at us as he once
did at Odysseus and the mariners imprisoned in his cave. He may have formed part of a
group representing the blinding of Polyphemus as prelude to the escape of Odysseus and
his companions.*

*References: Illustrated Handbook: Museum of Fine Arts, Boston, rev. ed. (Boston, 1964), pp. 86–87,
illus.; The Trojan War in Greek Art: A Picture Book (Boston, 1965), fig. 45; C. Vermeule, Classical Journal 60 (1965), 294–295, fig. 7.*

26

Sow at bay

Hellenistic; bronze; h. (max.) 0.10 m., l. (max.) 0.19 m.

William Francis Warden Fund. 64.510

The sow is rearing back slightly, her right front foot raised, as if to spring. She looks upwards, and her mouth is opened in a protective snarl. This master bronze may have been part of a group, a hunter and the hunted or a sow protecting her young. The adversary may have been a pack of dogs or a hunter on horseback. The animal's eyes are inlaid in silver and the fur and bristles are carefully cast and chasened. The surface patina is brown and green. Bronzes such as this were the delights of Alexander the Great's successors in the Hellenistic kingdoms from the Balkans to India. Roman generals, magistrates, and merchants inherited these tastes.

References: P. T. Rathbone, Museum of Fine Arts, Boston, *Annual Report, 1964* (Boston, 1965), 15; C. Vermeule, *Classical Journal* 61 (1966), 297, fig. 18, 302–303; M. Comstock and C. Vermeule, *Greek, Etruscan & Roman Bronzes in the Museum of Fine Arts, Boston* (Boston, 1971), p. 86, no. 92, 2 illus.

27

Medallions of Maximianus Herculeus
Roman, A.D. 306–307; gold; d. 33 m.
Theodora Wilbour Fund in memory of Zoë Wilbour. 59.495, 59.497

*The two medallions are part of a hoard of aurei and gold medallions dating to the
Tetrarch period. The obverses portray Maximianus wearing the lion's skin of Hercules
under whose protection he felt himself to be. One medallion, struck at Rome, has
Hercules standing on the reverse. The other, with the mint mark of Carthage, shows
Mars as protector of the imperial household. The medallions date to the second reign of
Maximianus in A.D. 306, when his son Maxentius was proclaimed emperor by the
troops in Rome and was joined by his father, who had previously abdicated in A.D. 305.
The portraits are superlative examples of the so-called cubist style in the Roman Empire
under Diocletian (284–305) and his colleagues the Tetrarchs.*

References: R. A. G. Carson, *Illustrated London News*, 14 November 1959, pp. 650–651, figs. 2–3;
M. Comstock and C. Vermeule, *Roman Medaillons* (Boston, 1963), pl. 9, nos. 84–85; G. Chase and
C. Vermeule, *Greek, Etruscan & Roman Art: The Classical Collections of the Museum of Fine
Arts, Boston*, rev. ed. (Boston, 1963), pp. 233, 271, figs. 271–272.

28

Late antique man of intellect, perhaps Saint Paul
Late Greek Imperial, ca. A.D. 400; Pentelic marble; h. 0.463 m.
J. H. and E. A. Payne Fund. 62.465

*Found at Agia Paraskevi in the surburbs of Athens, near an Early Christian basilica, this
man of powerful beard, piercing eyes, and large cranium is every inch a Greek philosopher or patriarch. He is a man of intellect and action. Head and neck were carved to be
let into a statue showing the subject standing, draped in a tunic and* pallium, *or*
himation. *A strong iconographic tradition in Late Graeco-Roman art suggests the awe-
some image could be Saint Paul, who preached in Athens. Otherwise, he was doubtless
a famous Greek magistrate or a renowned teacher in the schools of Athens.*

References: *Illustrated Handbook: Museum of Fine Arts, Boston* (Boston, 1964), rev. ed. pp. 98–99,
illus; C. Vermeule, *Classical Journal* 60 (1965), 302–303, fig. 17; C. Vermeule, *Roman Imperial
Art in Greece and Asia Minor* (Cambridge, Mass., 1968), pp. 365–369, fig. 183.

29

Head of a man

Roman, ca. A.D. 265–285; Proconnesian marble; h. 0.394 m.

Otis Norcross Fund. 58.1005

The portrait is executed in a style influenced by Antonine imperial heads of the later second century A.D., but the treatment of the eyes and beard point to the period from the last years of Gallienus to the reign of Carinus, about A.D. 265 to 285. The head may represent the emperor Marcus Aurelius Numerianus who died in Thrace in A.D. 284. Coin portraits providing the closest parallels belong to the last months of the emperor's life, and he was remembered as a gentle man of learning in an era of rough soldiers.

References: C. Vermeule, *Dumbarton Oaks Papers* 15, pp. 3 ff., figs. 1–6; G. M. A. Hanfmann, *Roman Art* (Greenwich, Conn., 1964), pp. 101–102, fig. 93, p. 184; H. von Heintze, *Roman Art* (New York, 1971), pp. 171, 183, 186, fig. 181.

44

30

Head of Socrates

Graeco-Roman, ca. A.D. 150; Pentelic marble; h. 0.204 m.

Frederick Brown Fund. 60.45

The portrait may be classed as Hellenistic in its naturalistic flavor. The head is an Antonine Roman version of a bronze statue by the great sculptor Lysippos, which shows Socrates seated in meditation, a work executed about 330 B.C., seventy years after the philosopher's death. The nose was broken and repaired in antiquity, for the iron dowel between the nostrils and the horizontal cutting above are ancient. This lifelike and expressive head appears to have been broken from a bust or herm.

References: C. Vermeule, *Classical Journal* 57 (1962), 156–167, fig. 15; G. Chase and C. Vermeule, *Greek, Etruscan & Roman Art: The Classical Collections in the Museum of Fine Arts, Boston,* rev. ed. (Boston, 1963), pp. 167–168, 179, fig. 159; G. M. A. Richter, *The Portraits of the Greeks* (London, 1965), p. 115, no. 24, figs. 519–521.

45

31

Fragments of a hanging
Eastern Mediterranean, probably sixth or seventh century; wool and linen, tapestry-woven; h. 184 cm., w. 93 cm.
Charles Potter Kling Fund. 57.180

The figure represented in these fragments of a large hanging or curtain is an ostiarius, or doorkeeper. This uniformed man holds back a curtain hanging between two columns. Over the columns is one arch and, to its right, a fragment of a second one, which suggests that the textile originally contained figures and architectural elements now lost. While the shading of the figure's tunic and hose gives a three-dimensional effect, a disregard for or misunderstanding of classical perspective and modeling renders his appearance awkward.

Reference: Larry Salmon, "An Eastern Mediterranean Puzzle," *Boston Museum Bulletin* 67 (1969), 136–150, figs. 1–6, 11, and cover.

II ASIATIC ART

32

Box

China, Late Eastern Chou period, ca. 3rd century B.C.; painted lacquer; h. 10.2 cm., diam. 26.7 cm.

Keith McLeod Fund. 68.696

The central medallion surrounded by three borders of geometric designs shows an open-mouthed dragon scratching his neck with his right front claw. Dragons of a similar type in various stages of stylization are shown on the walls of the lid and of the box. This piece probably came from Ch'ang-sha (Hunan province).

Reference: Max Loehr, "The Fate of the Ornament in Chinese Art," *Archives of Asian Art* 21 (1967–68), 12, figs. 9, 10.

33

Buddha with two attendant Bodhisattvas
India (Kashmir), 8th century; ivory; h. 12.2 cm.
Charles B. Hoyt, Marshall H. Gould and John Ware Willard Funds. 63.1495

The Buddha is seated in yogic posture between two Bodhisattvas. As is typical of Kash-
miri Buddhist art of the post-Gupta period, the sculpture shows iconographic influences
of both the Mathurā and the Gandhāra schools. However, the Gupta ideal of a smooth,
leonine torso with a concise and sober definition of the form has been retained. The
physiognomy is characteristically Kashmiri.

References: Milo Beach, "Two Indian Ivories Newly Acquired," Museum of Fine Arts, Boston,
Bulletin 62 (1964), 95–101. idem; "Indian and Islamic Objects Acquired by Robert Treat Paine,"
Museum of Fine Arts, Boston, *Bulletin* 63 (1965), 103–104; Jan Fontein and Pratapaditya Pal,
Museum of Fine Arts, Boston: Oriental Art (Boston, 1969), no. 122.

34

Seated Buddha and throne back
South India (Nagapattimam), ca. 9th century; gilt bronze; h. 81.9 cm.
Marshall H. Gould (throne back) and Keith McLeod (image) Funds. 1970.3

In December 1969 this seated image of a Buddha was reunited with the back of its throne. Two standing figures were originally attached to the back of the throne. No other South Indian Buddhist bronze of this style, size, and historical significance is known to exist.

References: The Arts of India and Nepal: The Nasli and Alice Heeramaneck Collection (Boston, 1966), no. 98 (throne back); *Centennial Acquisitions,* special issue of the *Boston Museum Bulletin* 68 (1970), 39–40, no. 20.

35

Lokanātha

India (Bihār), 11th century; gray schist; h. 88.9 cm.

Marshall H. Gould and Frederick L. Jack Funds. 63.418

Seated in princely posture, the Bodhisattva holds a lotus stem with his left hand; the right hand, now broken, probably displayed the gesture of exposition (vyākhyāna-mudrā). A work of the mature Pāla style, the sculpture is probably from the Bishenpur-Tandawa region of Bihār. Stylistically, the sculpture represents the transition between the soft but crisp and taut modeling of the mature Pāla style and the langorous but effete grace of later works of the Sena period.

References: Milo Beach, "Indian and Islamic Objects Acquired by Robert Treat Paine," Museum of Fine Arts, Boston, *Bulletin* 63 (1965), 103, illus. p. 105; Jan Fontein and Pratapaditya Pal, *Museum of Fine Arts, Boston: Oriental Art* (Boston, 1969), no. 127.

36

Milkmaids in a garden
India (Rājasthān), late 17th century; painting on cotton; 244 × 264 cm.
Gift of John Goelet. 67.837

Beneath flowering trees, teeming with squirrels, parrots, and peacocks, stand six women.
The row of cows in the bottom frieze suggests that they are milkmaids (gopīs), the
companions of Krishna. At the top in the clouds are the gods riding their heavenly
mounts. The entire scene, arranged in a strictly symmetrical fashion, is surrounded by a
band of floral scrolls.

37

Cover

India (Golconda?), 1630–1700; cotton, painted and treated with mordants, resist medium, and dyes; h. 67 cm., w. 82 cm.

Gift of John Goelet. 66.230

The field shows peris, mythical beings, dancing and playing instruments. Gazelle-like animals lie among the rocks in the lower left corner, and appear elsewhere in the field, with birds, hares, plants and trees. The border shows an arabesque of polychrome leaves and medallions.

Reference: Museum of Fine Arts, Boston, *The Arts of India and Nepal: The Nasli and Alice Heeramaneck Collection* (Boston, 1966), 168, pl. 250.

38

Bowl

Persia (Gurgan), dated in accordance with A.D. 1284; ceramic; h. 8.9 cm., diam. 19.5 cm. Gift of the John Goelet Foundation. 65.232

The bowl luster is painted with a lion design in the center. The inscription on the inside rim is executed in a goldish tone, and the rim and outside edge are in a more reddish luster.

54

39
Bowl
Persia, first half of the 14th century; ceramic (Sultanabad ware); h. 9.5 cm., diam. 19 cm.
Charles B. Hoyt Fund. 65.1669

The interior shows a resting doe in a central medallion, surrounded by four foliage medallions separated by flying birds. The bowl is painted in gray green with some lavender on a white ground.

Reference: Museum of Fine Arts, Boston, *The Museum Year: 1965* (Boston, 1966), 47.

40

Carpet

Persia, 1525–1550; silk, silver, and gilt silver; knotted pile (sehna) and brocading; l. 480 cm., w. 255 cm.

Gift of John Goelet, Centennial Purchase Fund, and restricted funds. 66.293

Mounted riders portrayed in hunting scenes dominate the field of this carpet. The quatrefoil medallion in the center shows pairs of phoenixes attacking single dragons. A rich garden fills the borders, in which appear seated figures and their attendants.

The ground fabric and pile are made entirely of silk yarns, and each square inch contains approximately 728 to 812 knots. In addition, silk yarns wrapped with flat silver or gilt silver wires have been brocaded into the ground fabric in many places. It is believed that the carpet was woven in a court manufactory, probably at Kashan in central Persia. Only two carpets of this particular type, with figures in the borders and made entirely of silk, have survived. The other example is in the Österreichisches Museum für angewandte Kunst in Vienna.

Collections: Marchese Torrigiani; Stefano Bardini; Baron Adolphe de Rothschild; Baron Maurice de Rothschild.

References: Friedrich Sarre and Hermann Trenkwald, *Old Oriental Carpets* (Vienna: Österreichisches Museum für Kunst und Industrie, 1929), vol. 2, pls. 24–26; *Boston Museum Bulletin* 69 (1971), 1–87, figs. 1–8, I–V, frontispiece and cover.

41

Elephant

Persia (Gurgan?), 12th century; ceramic; h. 33.9 cm., w. 23 cm.
Keith McLeod Fund. 65.1271

This elephant with howdah, rider, and driver was painted with black under turquoise glaze and engraved. Such elephants are rather rare in Persian ceramics, and this is an outstanding example of a ceramic object whose function was purely decorative. Although the legs are straight and pillarlike, and the head and trunk rather disproportionate, the artist has well expressed the sense of volume and elemental power of the animal.

References: Museum of Fine Arts, Boston, *The Museum Year: 1965* (Boston, 1966), 47; Jan Fontein and Pratapaditya Pal, *Museum of Fine Arts, Boston: Oriental Art* (Boston, 1969), no. 130.

42

Dainichi Nyorai

Japan, 11th century; wood; h. 55.5 cm., w. 40.2 cm., d. 28.4 cm.

Keith McLeod Fund. 1970.61

This statue of Dainichi Nyorai is a multiple-block construction (yosegi) with an almost completely original coat of lacquer. The hands are in the Wisdom Fist gesture (chiken-in).

Reference: Museum of Fine Arts, Boston, *The Museum Year: 1969–70* (Boston, 1970), 35–36.

43

Cosmetic box

Korea, Koryo period, 10th–11th century; gilt silver; h. 6.9 cm., l. 26.5 cm., w. 11.8 cm.
Keith McLeod Fund. 63.1610

On an oval in the center of the cover a figure of a crane with outspread wings and tail stands holding a leaf-shaped ornament in its beak. The bird's body and tail are overlaid with lines and loops of twisted wire. Suspended from the twisted wire attached to the sides of the box are leaf ornaments, four of which are modern replacements. Cloud forms are depicted on the bottom of the box by raised dots in repoussé. The sides of the box and cover are held together by metal strips attached with small, evenly spaced rivets.

References: Jan Fontein and Rose Hempel, *China-Korea-Japan* (Berlin, 1968), pl. XXXII; Robert Treat Paine, "Some Recent Accessions," Museum of Fine Arts, Boston, *Bulletin* 62 (1964), 123.

44

CHAO LING-JANG, Chinese, flourished 1080–ca. 1100
Summer Mist along the Lake Shore
Sung period, A.D. 1100; handscroll, ink and colors on silk; h. 19.1 cm., l. 161.3 cm.
Keith McLeod Fund. 57.724

As a typical representative of the landscape painters of the Academy of K'ai-feng, Chao Ling-jang depicts a misty landscape in which geese are the only living beings. No steep mountains rise up, for the painter's intention was to evoke the atmosphere of the plains in the vicinity of the capital. This scroll, signed and dated in accordance with A.D. 1100, is one of the rare paintings generally accepted as a work of this master.

References: Jan Fontein and Pratapaditya Pal, *Museum of Fine Arts, Boston: Oriental Art*
(Boston, 1969), no. 96; Seiichi Taki, "Extant Paintings of the Northern Sung Period," *Kokka,*
no. 494 (1932), 3–14.

45

Flask (pien-hu)

China, Ming dynasty, mark and period of Hsüan-tê (1426–1435); porcelain; h. 29 cm., w. 20.6 cm. and 12.9 cm.

Gift of Horace Morison. 56.50

The gourd-shaped flask has two loop handles. The upper bulb is decorated with a band of floral scrolls. Below on both sides is a rosette surrounded by a band of foliate scroll. The entire decoration is in underglaze blue.

Reference: Jean Gordon Lee, "An Exhibition of Blue-Decorated Porcelain of the Ming Dynasty," *Philadelphia Museum Bulletin* 44 (1949), no. 32.

46

CHU TA, Chinese, 1625–after 1705
Lotus in the Manner of Hsü Wei
17th century; ink on paper; 18.5 × 89.8 cm.
Keith McLeod. 56.495

*This work is painted in the style of Hsü Wei, one
of the great eccentrics of the Ming period who
specialized in monochrome paintings of plants
and birds. The poem inscribed on the painting
seems to contain an oblique reference to the fall of
the Ming dynasty.*

References: Jan Fontein and Pratapaditya Pal, *Museum
of Fine Arts, Boston: Oriental Art* (Boston, 1969),
no. 100; Kojiro Tomita and Hsien-ch'i Tseng, *Portfolio
of Chinese Paintings in the Museum: Yuan to Ch'ing
Periods* (Boston, 1961), pl. 121.

III MEDIEVAL ART

47

Chalice of Saint Stephen

East Greek, A.D. 525–575; silver with gold and niello inlay; h. 0.18 m., w. (at handles) 0.266 m., w. (bowl) 0.16 m.

Edward J. and Mary S. Holmes Fund. 1971.633

The form and especially the handles of this Early Christian or Eastern Imperial (Byzantine) votive vessel derive from Hellenistic Greek metalwork. A large Christogram ("Chi Rho" the first letters of Christ) flanked by an "Alpha" and an "Omega" are inlaid on either side. The inscription in good Roman Imperial Greek letters within the frieze between the handles reads "Sarah prayed and made (this) offering to the First Martyr." He was, of course, the deacon who was stoned to death, Saint Stephen.

48

Virgin and Child

Italy (Lombardy), late 12th century; polychromed limestone; h. 73.6 cm., w. 40 cm., d. 21.9 cm.

Maria Antoinette Evans Fund. 57.583

The Madonna clasps her Child, inclining her head as He draws near to her. The formula for this representation is Byzantine (glykophilousa, sweetly loving Mother of God). The profound tenderness expressed in this work surpasses formula and betrays genuine sympathy and understanding for the subject.

The anonymous artist has been identified as the one responsible for the reliefs in Castellarquato near Modena. The figures are both clothed and organized by linear ornamental systems, as is conventional in the twelfth century. But the particular beauty of these systems, of the form and line of the group and of the handling of the finished back of the statue indicate the work of an extraordinarily gifted sculptor.

References: Hanns Swarzenski, "A Masterpiece of Lombard Sculpture," Museum of Fine Arts, Boston, *Bulletin* 57 (1959), 64–75; Walter Cahn, "Romanesque Sculpture in American Collections, VI, The Boston Museum of Fine Arts," *Gesta* 9 (1970), 69 f., no. 12; Hanns Swarzenski in *Museum of Fine Arts, Boston: Western Art* (Boston, 1971), no. 37.

49

Oliphant
Italy (Salerno?), ca. 1100; ivory; l. 68 cm.
Maria Antoinette Evans Fund. 57.581

*Medieval man spun a web of mystery, legend, and wonder when he considered ele-
phants and their precious product, ivory. Legend attached itself to the great horns called
oliphants, which originally served various purposes such as hunting, as containers for
drink, and as contractual symbols in the transfer of land (tenure horns). Some found
their way into church treasuries because they were associated with saints and venera-
ted as relics or because they were containers for relics. The richer of two medieval
oliphants in Boston, this horn is the product of a workshop possibly responsible for
similar works now in Paris, Vienna, York, and other collections. Animals, mythical
beasts, Hercules and the hind, and rich ornament combine to produce an exotic marriage
of western and eastern spirit and imagery.*

Reference: Hanns Swarzenski, "Two Oliphants in the Museum," Museum of Fine Arts, Boston,
Bulletin 60 (1962), 27–45.

66

50

Aquamanile in the form of a human bust
Lower Saxony (Magdeburg?), late 13th century; bronze; h. 24.2 cm., w. 18.1 cm., d. 17.2 cm.
Decorative Arts Special Fund. 65.465

*Pouring vessels of this kind are much rarer than those made in the shape of lions and
other beasts. But the "humanization" of even such purely utilitarian objects is highly
characteristic of the spirit of the period. The type is obviously inspired by classical
drinking vessels and Byzantine weights made in the form of a bust. Other sources of
inspiration are the western Romanesque reliquaries portraying the head of the saint
whose bones are enshrined in it. This bust, depicting a praying man in the same way as
the Early Christian Church depicted an "Orans," was made in one of the leading
bronze foundries of Lower Saxony, probably Magdeburg, for export to the newly
Christianized countries east of the Elbe, especially Poland and Russia. In fact, the vessel
was dug up in Borsow from the Dniester River. Scratched lines at the eyebrows and below
the almond-shaped eyes, as well as the hatched dots indicating the stubbles of the beard,
seem to be characteristic of a series of contemporary bronzes located at Magdeburg. The
bust, compelling in its "archaic" strength and monumentality, is a telling example of
the northern Romanesque Renaissance.*

References: Sale Catalog Helbring, Munich, 5–7 November 1931, no. 73; Otto von Falke and
E. Meyer, *Bronzegeräte des Mittelalters* (Berlin, 1935), no. 335, fig. 312.

51

Virgin and Child

France (Île-de-France), ca. 1200; oak, gesso, polychromed and gilt; h. 1.55 m., w. 63.5 cm., d. 39.4 cm.

William F. Warden Fund. 59.701

Tu thronus es Salamonis	Thou art the Throne of Solomon
cui nullus par thronis	To which among all thrones not one is equal
Arte vel materia	Either in art or material

In this way Adam of St. Victor (died 1180) described the Virgin as the Throne of Solomon, the seat of wisdom. Solomon was seen as the prefiguration of Christ; Christ was held to be the embodiment of wisdom. It has been convincingly shown that this stately, elongated figure bears striking stylistic analogies with the figures decorating the north transept at Chartres. Exceptional quality informs the execution of every detail: the rich drapery, which falls in deep folds and eddies about the Virgin's feet; the ornament drawn from the goldsmith's repertoire that decorates the throne.

References: Hanns Swarzenski, "*A Vierge d'Orée,*" Museum of Fine Arts, Boston, *Bulletin* 58 (1960), 64–83; Hanns Swarzenski in *Museum of Fine Arts, Boston: Western Art* (Boston, 1971), no. 40.

68

52 *(detail, p. 69)*
St. John
Italy (Tuscany?), 14th century; polychromed poplar (feet are modern replacements);
h. 72.7 cm., d. 31.7 cm.
Centennial Purchase Fund. 67.767

The figure of St. John is the only known survivor of a monumental Crucifixion group,
which would have included the Crucified Christ and the Mourning Virgin. Indeed,
this powerful statue projects through facial expression and the gesture of the hands the
quiet but intense pathos of Christ's death upon the Cross. The massive drapery is caught
up in the front and organized at the side in great triangular folds – stylistic hallmarks
that will one day, it is hoped, identify other works by this Gothic master and further
identify a great artistic personality.

Reference: Centennial Acquisitions, special issue of *Boston Museum Bulletin* 68 (1970), 52–53,
no. 52.

70

53 *(detail, p. 72)*
Tapestry hanging: Wild Men and Moors
South Germany, region of Alsace, possibly Strasbourg, ca. 1400; wool and linen, tapestry-woven; h. 100 cm., w. 490 cm.
Charles Potter Kling Fund. 54.1431

Wild men, as depicted in this tapestry, were a favorite medieval theme in literature and the arts. In this tapestry-weaving a group of wild men attack a castle; some are in combat with a lion, a dragon, and a unicorn, and others gather around a wild woman and two children. The facial features are not woven but are painted on with thin washes. At the lower edge three helmets with crests and mantlings, and one heraldic shield are shown, representing the Zorn and Blümel families, both of Strasbourg.

The acquisition of this tapesty by the museum was supported by Mr. Rathbone while he was director elect.

Collections: Prince Hohenzollern-Sigmaringen; Fürstlich Hohenzollernsches Museum, Sigmaringen; Othmar Straus.

References: Adolph S. Cavallo, *Tapestries of Europe and of Colonial Peru in the Museum of Fine Arts, Boston* (Boston, 1967), vol. I, pp. 47–49; vol. 2, pls. 1, 1 a–1 f; Gertrude Townsend, "A South German Tapestry," Museum of Fine Arts, Boston, *Bulletin* 56 (1958), 5–17, fig. 1 and cover.

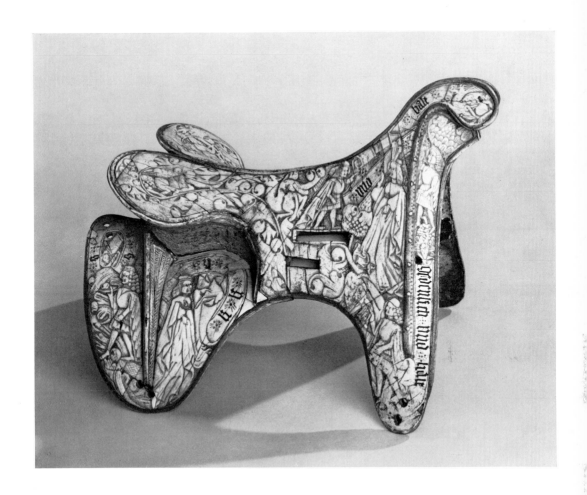

54

Knightly saddle

Austria (Tyrol?), ca. 1450; polychromed staghorn, birch bark; h. 35.6 cm., l. 45.7 cm., d. 30.5 cm.

Centennial Purchase Fund. 69.944

The elaborate carving and bright coloring probably indicate that this saddle, one of twenty that survive, was used for special occasions, although the pattern of wear also suggests considerable use. A prized object, in any case, the saddle appears to have belonged to a noble Hungarian family from at least 1520 until shortly before its inclusion in our collection. Secular motifs, courtly figures reminiscent of those found in contemporary German prints, dragons, other grotesques, and foliate ornament cover the entire surface, giving a rich effect. To underline the liveliness of the whole, and as if in appreciation of the shape, the artist has outlined the edges in red. The inscription aptly warns "Gedenkch und halt" ("Think before you leap")! Perhaps as added precaution, a tiny cross was inscribed on a shield just below the pommel.

References: John F. Hayward, "A Fifteenth Century Carved Bone Saddle," *Auction* 2 (March 1969), 22–23; *Centennial Acquisitions*, special issue of *Boston Museum Bulletin* 68 (1970), 58, no. 34.

55

Master of the Gardens of Love, Netherlandish, active 1440–1450
The Little Garden of Love
Engraving; 8.5 × 19.8 cm.
Katherine Eliot Bullard Fund. 65.594

Any print room is delighted to acquire a unique fifteenth-century print. But rarity and charm are seldom joined together as they are in this small print. Twenty-one engravings have been attributed to the Master of the Gardens of Love, each of them surviving in a single impression. The engraver is believed to have been a goldsmith active about 1440–1450, and he was certainly strongly influenced by the artistic climate of Burgundy during the reign of Philip the Good. In this print, various kinds of courtly love are taking place in the presence of the Queen of Love. A literary source is suggested as well as the flavor of a Burgundian court pageant.

References: Max Lehrs, *Geschichte und kritischer Katalog des deutschen, niederländischen und französischen Kupferstichs im XV Jahrhundert* (Vienna, 1908), vol. I, no. 20; Henry P. Possiter, "The Little Garden of Love," Museum of Fine Arts, Boston, *Bulletin* 63 (1965), 197–202.

56

MASTER OF THE AMSTERDAM CABINET (The Housebook Master), German, active last quarter of 15th century
Mother with Two Children and a Blank Shield
Bearded Man with a Blank Shield
Drypoint; each 9.5×7.3 cm.
Katherine Eliot Bullard Fund. 66.375, 66.376

Ever since its founding eighty-five years ago the Print Department had hoped to have the Master of the Amsterdam Cabinet represented in its collections, and in 1966 two superb examples of his work were acquired. Many of his prints exist in single impressions, and most of these are owned by the Rijksprentenkabinet of the Rijksmuseum, Amsterdam, which gave its name to this early German engraver. The museum's Mother with Two Children and a Blank Shield *is a unique impression, and the* Bearded Man with a Blank Shield *is one of five examples. Both the artist's direct, lively observation of the real world and his technique greatly influenced the work of Albrecht Dürer.*

References: Max Lehrs, *Geschichte und kritischer Katalog des deutschen, niederländischen und französischen Kupferstichs im XV Jahrhundert* (Vienna, 1932), vol. 8, nos. 84, 85; Henry P. Rossiter, "The Master of the Amsterdam Cabinet," *Boston Museum Bulletin* 64 (1966), 173–177.

57

Virgin and Child on the Crescent Moon
Lower Austria, ca. 1450–1460; polychromed and gilt poplar; h. 1.78 m., w. 50.2 cm.,
d. 21.6 cm.
Centennial Purchase Fund. 65.1354

Carved from a single piece of wood, and retaining most of its original polychromy and gilding, the Austrian Virgin, presented as the Apocalyptic Virgin standing on the Moon, is one of the finest extant examples of the Gothic type of "Schoenen Madonnen." The image of the wide-eyed gangling Child, however, far from the infant-ruler type of the earlier middle ages, gives the group a compelling and intimate human quality that contrasts with the remote beauty of the figure of the Virgin. Late Gothic realism characterizes the expressive features of the moon and also the drapery, organized in deep angular folds that underline the gentle sway of the Virgin as Queen.

Reference: *Centennial Acquisitions,* special issue of *Boston Museum Bulletin* 68 (1970), 53, no. 30.

58

Portrait bust

Austria (Salzburg), ca. 1500; glazed and polychromed Hafner ware; h. 59 cm., w. 40 cm., d. 23 cm.

Gift of R. Thornton Wilson in memory of John Fitzgerald Kennedy, Thirty-fifth President of the United States. 64.1

Certainly remarkable as a rare late Gothic portrait in sculpture, this unique bust is even more astounding for its depth of expression, for the mood of sorrow yet resignation that the figure projects so strongly. (In its capacity to communicate feeling, the portrait invites comparison with Kokoschka's self-portrait, no. 113 in this exhibition). The bust is executed in materials and techniques traditionally applied to elaborate ornamental stoves, tiles, and vessels during this period in Germany, Austria, and Switzerland – fired earthenware and varieties of tin and lead glazes. It is known that the figure once stood in a wayside chapel near Gars, in Upper Bavaria, although we have no precise information concerning its previous history. It has been suggested that the bust is a self-portrait of a Hafner master.

References: Hanns Swarzenski, "Masterpiece of Northern Portrait Sculpture, A Memorial to President Kennedy," Museum of Fine Arts, Boston, *Bulletin* 61 (1963), 143–148; Hanns Swarzenski in *Museum of Fine Arts, Boston: Western Art* (Boston, 1971), no. 43.

59

Tapestry hanging: Narcissus
France or the Franco-Flemish territories, late fifteenth or early sixteenth century; wool and silk, tapestry-woven; h. 282 cm., w. 311 cm.
Charles Potter Kling Fund. 68.114

The designer of this tapestry has placed the handsome young Narcissus by a fountain, regarding his reflection in the water. In this millefleurs *("thousand flowers") tapestry, myriad plants, birds, and beasts cover the ground. Of all surviving examples of* mille-fleur *tapestries, this is the only one showing a subject derived from Ovid's* Metamorphoses.

IV RENAISSANCE & BAROQUE ART

60

FLEMISH, 15th century

Triptych:

Martyrdom of Saint Hippolytus

Outer Wings:

St. Bavo of Ghent, St. Elizabeth of Hungary, St. Thomas à Becket,
St. Catherine of Alexandria and arms of the donors, Berthos and his
wife, née Kleverwyck

Oil on panel; 100.4×292.1 cm. over all.

Walter M. Cabot Fund. 63.660

In a state of near-perfect preservation, this triptych, completely unknown before it was
acquired by the Boston Museum, is one of the most important works of art to come to
the museum in the last decade. Its painter still unknown, this triptych bears an un-
deniable connection with the Bouts altarpiece of the same subject at Saint-Sauveur,
Bruges. The left wing of that altarpiece, painted by Hugo van der Goes, depicts Hippo-
lytus de Berthos and his wife, who also commissioned the Boston triptych.

Collections: Emile Gavet, Paris; Claude Lafontaine, Paris.

References: Sale Catalogue, Palais Galliera (Collection Claude Lafontaine), 11 April 1962,, no. 14;
Perry T. Rathbone in *Museum of Fine Arts, Boston: Western Art* (Boston, 1971), no. 98.

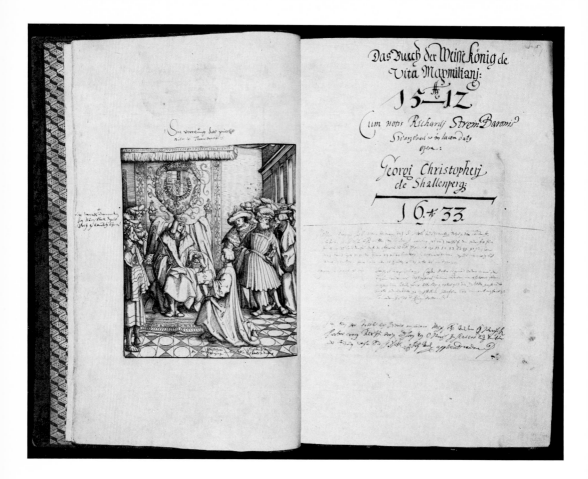

61

Maximilian I's *Weisskunig* (Liechtenstein Codex G)
"Presentation of the Book to the Emperor"
Woodcut, proof impression by HANS BURGKMAIR, German, 1473–1531. Page h. 42.3 cm.
The facing page with notes in various hands and the manuscript title added by a seven-
teenth-century owner of the codex.
Katherine Eliot Bullard Fund. 57.40

*Maximilian I, Emperor of the Holy Roman Empire from 1494 to 1518, planned and
partly wrote* Der Weisskunig *(The White King), an illustrated political history of his
reign, told as an epic romance. The enterprise was never completed and published, but
the museum is fortunate to have acquired the Liechtenstein Codex, one of four albums
of drawings and woodcuts that were intended for the book. Our volume contains 119
proof impressions of woodcuts by Hans Burgkmair and Leonard Beck, 52 pen drawings
for unexecuted woodcuts, notations above some of the woodcuts in Maximilian's own
hand, and a transcript of a letter from Maximilian to one of his advisers regarding the
project. The volume is a rich supplement to the museum's collection of prints by
Albrecht Dürer and other artists who worked for Maximilian.*

References: Alvin Schultz, "Der Weisskunig," *Jahrbuch der kunsthistorischen Sammlungen des
allerhöchsten Kaiserhauses* (1888); Museum of Fine Arts, Boston, *Annual Report, 1957* (Boston,
1958), pp. 55–56; *Boston Museum Bulletin* 65 (1967), 118, no. 16.

62

ALBRECHT DÜRER, German, 1471–1528
The Fall of Man (Adam and Eve)
1504; engraving (Bartsch 1, Meder 1, II, a); 25.2 × 19.5 cm.
Centennial Gift of Landon T. Clay. 68.187

The Print Department has adhered well to the precepts of its first curator, Sylvester R. Koehler. He believed that a large print room should contain impressions of varying quality, and thus many so-called duplicates have been retained. The addition in 1968 of nearly one hundred Dürer prints from the Tomás Harris collection makes the museum's group of Dürers stand as a splendid tribute to Koehler's principle. These prints provide a fine teaching tool, frequently used, and were exhibited to the public in 1971 in an exceptionally well-received exhibition that drew over 35,000 viewers.

The magnificently proportioned, ideal forms of man and woman are deftly lighted so as to stand out against minutely observed plants and animals which also have symbolic meanings related to the nature of man.

References: Joseph Meder, *Dürer-Katalog* (Vienna, 1932); Erwin Panofsky, *Albrecht Dürer* (Princeton, 1943); Museum of Fine Arts, Boston, *Albrecht Dürer: Master Printmaker* (Boston, 1971), no. 84.

63

ALBRECHT DÜRER, German, 1471–1528
The Abduction
1516; etching (Bartsch 72, Meder 67); 31 × 21.5 cm.
Katherine Eliot Bullard Fund. 68.208

Dürer is experimenting with a new technique – etching. He represents an unidentified subject that contrasts in its wildness to the still beauty of Adam and Eve.

References: Joseph Meder, *Dürer-Katalog* (Vienna, 1932); Erwin Panofsky, *Albrecht Dürer* (Princeton, 1943); Museum of Fine Arts, Boston, *Albrecht Dürer: Master Printmaker* (Boston, 1971), no. 194.

The woodcut inscription reads: QVI VVLT POST ME VENIRE ABNEGET SEMET IPSVM ET TOLLAT CRVCEM SVA ET SEQVAT ME

64

ANONYMOUS, Milanese, 1500
Christ Bearing the Cross
Woodcut, hand colored; 55.2 × 42 cm.
Katherine Eliot Bullard Fund. 63.2668

The museum's collection of early Italian prints is outstanding, and this striking and well-preserved woodcut acquired in 1963 is an important addition. The only other known impression, printed in a grayish black ink and much restored, is in the Berlin Print Room. The subject also exists in a second version from a block cut in a deceptively similar style. Schreiber believed it to be a later state of the woodcut, lacking both the inscription and borderline and signed with the monogram of the sixteenth-century cutter Andrea Andreani. This alternate woodblock, very worn, came into the possession of the Academy of Fine Arts, Modena. Modern impressions, without the monogram, were printed, and the museum also owns one of these.

References: Friedich Lippmann, *The Art of Woodengraving in Italy in the XVth Century* (London, 1888), p. 169; W. L. Schreiber, *Handbuch der Holz- und Metallschnitte des XV Jahrhunderts* (Leipzig, 1926), vol. 2, 919ᴵ.

87

65

FRA BARTOLOMMEO, Italian, 1475–1517
Farm buildings and pollarded mulberry tree (recto)
Farm buildings and water mill (verso)
Probably 1500–1510; pen and brown ink; 28.7 × 21.6 cm.
Francis Bartlett Fund. 58.1

Forty-one landscape drawings by Fra Bartolommeo, formed into an album in the eighteenth century, were discovered in England and sold at auction in 1957. Previous to this, only four landscape drawings by the Renaissance painter had been known. Although the museum has no funds designated specifically for drawings, Mr. Rathbone has encouraged the acquisition of important drawings. With his assistance, general funds were procured, and the museum was fortunately able to purchase this double-sided sheet with its pruned tree and delicately drawn farm buildings in the sunlit Italian countryside. It is unique among the group in that on the verso is the only figure study in the album.

References: Museum of Fine Arts, Boston, *Bulletin* 56 (1958), 106–108; *Sotheby Sale Catalogue*, 20 November 1957, lot 5.

88

66

Lucas van Leyden, Dutch, 1494–1533
Moses Striking the Rock
Tempera on canvas; inscribed "L 1527"; 183 × 236 cm.
William K. Richardson Fund. 54.1432

A major figure in northern Renaissance art, Lucas van Leyden was principally an engraver. His paintings, therefore, are few, and dated examples are even rarer, there being only two others of his mature years extant, one in the Hermitage and the other in the Leiden Museum. Moses Striking the Rock *is the only known work on canvas by this artist. His exquisite draftsmanship is evident in the painting, which shows the strong influence of contemporary Venetian painting. The interpretation of the textual source, Exodus 17 : 3–6, is unusual, in that the artist has chosen to depict the distribution of the water by Moses rather than the more dramatic moment of the miracle itself. The painting was perhaps acquired by Camillo Borghese (1550–1620), later Pope Paul V, as it was observed in the Villa Borghese in 1657; it was acquired from the family in 1896 by the Germanisches Nationalmuseum in Nuremberg. The purchase by our museum was made possible by the enthusiastic support of Mr. Rathbone, director elect.*

References: Max J. Friedländer, *Die Altniederländische Malerei* (Leiden, 1932), vol. 10, p. 99, no. 116, p. 135; idem, *Lucas van Leyden* (Berlin, 1963), p. 66; Perry T. Rathbone in *Museum of Fine Arts, Boston: Western Art* (Boston, 1971), no. 134.

67

Hour glass

England, 1525–1550; glass, gilt silver, cast, stamped and chased; w. 17.8 cm.
Theodora Wilbour Fund in memory of Charlotte Beebe Wilbour. 57.533

This elegant instrument is one of the few silver-mounted hour glasses to survive from the Renaissance period and may be one of the earliest. The designer of the piece was ingenious as well as extremely tasteful. A simple locking device at the end of each arm of the scroll-decorated frame allows the glass to be reversed to repeat the movement by changing the point of attachment of the glass frame to the ornamental frame. The sophisticated chased decoration, though common in Northern Europe in the sixteenth century, is composed, applied, and executed in such a masterly way that some authors have suggested that the hour glass may have been designed by Hans Holbein while working at the court of Henry VIII.

Reference: John David Farmer, *The Virtuoso Craftsman: Northern European Design in the Sixteenth Century* (Worcester, 1969), no. 8.

90

68

BENVENUTO DI GIOVANNI, Italian, 1436–ca. 1518

Expulsion from Paradise

Tempera on panel; 25.5 × 34 cm.

Charles Potter Kling Fund. 56.512

Although this predella panel had been attributed to Girolamo di Benvenuto (1470–1524) and Cosimo Tura (ca. 1430–1495), Bernard Berenson's acceptance of it in 1932 as a work by Benvenuto di Giovanni remains undisputed. Unfortunately, no other portions of the altarpiece are presently known. This beautiful little panel, full of emotional spirit, is iconographically unusual in that an angel forcibly leads Adam and Eve by the hand from the Garden of Eden, and it adds to the somewhat sparse representation of fifteenth-century Sienese painting in the museum's collection. Less than a dozen works in the United States are credited to Benvenuto di Giovanni.

References: Bernard Berenson, *Italian Pictures of the Renaissance* (Oxford, 1932), p. 77 (listed with Mme. Emile Paravicini, Paris); Thomas N. Maytham, "An Expulsion from Paradise by Benvenuto di Giovanni," Museum of Fine Arts, Boston, *Bulletin* 55 (1957), 44–46.

69

Infant Hercules Wrestling with the Serpents
Italy (Florence), early 16th century; bronze; h. 22.9 cm.
John Goelet Departmental Fund. 68.617

Small bronzes such as this, inspired by classical statuary and subject matter, illustrate the fascination that the antique held for Italian artists and collectors of the fifteenth and sixteenth centuries – fascination to the point that bronze reductions were made of new pieces of ancient statuary as they were discovered. Here the infant Hercules is shown in a pose which is less a violent struggle, more an essay on a mobile anatomy, and an excuse for a composition superbly finished by the coiling of the serpent up the arm of the figure. There are other casts in Berlin, Staatliche Museen, and Vienna, ex-Benda Collection.

Reference: Christie's Sale Catalogue (The Henry Oppenheimer Collection), 15 July 1936, no. 116.

70

Centaur Attacked by a Lion
Italy (Florence?), ca. 1540; bronze; h. 28 cm.
Gift of Jack Linsky. 64.2218

Unattributed, apparently unique, this bronze poses perhaps unanswerable questions. What is sure is that the statue is, as far as quality and technique are concerned, a virtuoso piece. From conception to rough cast to highly finished state, the piece was the work of a master, in whose hands chisels and fine engraving tools produced effects usually confined to goldsmith's work. Color, chiseling, and finishing can stand for the best of what is possible in the making of bronze statuary.

92

71

PIER JACOPO ALARI BONACOLSI (called "ANTICO"), Italian, ca. 1460–1528
Cleopatra
Ca. 1500; bronze, partly gilt; h. 64.5 cm., w. 48.9 cm.
William F. Warden Fund. 64.2174

With the acquisition of this bust, the museum added an undeniable masterpiece to a small but select collection of renaissance bronzes. Possibly identifiable with a bust mentioned in a seventeenth-century inventory of the Gonzaga family in Mantua, our piece is identical in style, size, and finish with life-size busts of Bacchus and Ariadne in the Kunsthistorisches Museum, Vienna. All three were perhaps made for the Studiolo of Isabella d'Este in Mantua, seat of the Gonzagas, famous at this time as a humanistic center. Heavily indebted to classical art, as is all of Antico's surviving work, this piece somehow projects a softness and quality of mood that sets it apart from the Vienna busts and the majority of the master's work. The entire figure is superbly modeled and finished with a crispness, precision, and detail, which once included the earrings attached to the pierced ears.

References: Hermann Julius Hermann, Essay in *Jahrbuch der Sammlungen des allerhöchsten Kaiserhauses* 28 (Vienna, 1909–10), 279; Detlef Heikamp, *L'Antico,* I Maestri della Scultura (Milano, 1966), fig. XIV, XV.

72

Small cover with an unidentified coat of arms
Peru, Colonial period, late sixteenth century or seventeenth century; silk, linen, and cotton, tapestry-woven; h. 45 cm., w. 42 cm.
Charles Potter Kling Fund. 60.794

The museum owns at present one of the most extensive collections of Peruvian colonial tapestry weavings in the world. This cover is unique among the museum's examples in that the pattern is woven almost entirely of silk yarns. Silk was introduced in Peru by the Spaniards and was only rarely used this extensively by the Peruvians.

Reference: Adolph S. Cavallo, *Tapestries of Europe and of Colonial Peru in the Museum of Fine Arts, Boston* (Boston, 1967), vol. 1, pp. 189–191; vol. 2, pl. 57.

73

Attributed to ADRIAEN DE VRIES, Dutch, ca. 1560–1629

Naiad

Ca. 1620; terra cotta, patinated; h. 35.6 cm.

Hezekiah E. Bolles Fund. 56.144

An exceptionally fine addition to the museum's important collection of sculptor's models, the figure of a naiad may be a working design for a fountain project or possibly a study for a bronze group, which is suggested by the high finish and color of the piece. The fine modeling of the head and the general style recall the powerful tradition of Giovanni da Bologna, so influential upon northern sculptors of the period such as de Vries and Hubert Gerhard.

Collection: Oskar Bondy, Vienna.

74

IL ROSSO FIORENTINO, Italian, 1494–1540
Dead Christ with Angels
Ca. 1524–1527; oil on panel signed "Rubeus Flo"; 133.5 × 104 cm.
Charles Potter Kling Fund. 58.527

This great masterpiece, whose whereabouts had been unknown for generations, came
form the collection of Christine de Bourbon, Madrid. It is the greatest Italian mannerist
painting in this country. It was executed in Rome for Cardinal Leonardo Tournabuoni,
Bishop of Borgo San Sepolcro in Umbria and a close friend of Rosso. It is one of only
fifteen to twenty easel paintings accepted as by the artist. The work shows the strong
influence of Michelangelo and the antique.

References: Vasari, *Le Vite de 'piu eccellenti pittori, scrittori ed architettori* (ed. 1550), vol. 2,
p. 800; John Shearman, "The Dead Christ by Rosso Fiorentino," *Boston Museum Bulletin* 64
(1966), 148 ff.; Perry T. Rathbone in *Museum of Fine Arts, Boston: Western Art* (Boston, 1971),
no. 135.

75

JACQUES BELLANGE, French, active 1602–1616
The Raising of Lazarus
Etching, second state; 46.0×31.2 cm.
Gift of Lydia Evans Tunnard in memory of W. G. Russell Allen. 63.2780

The elegant, languid figures with their mannered poses and expressive gestures are characteristic of this French artist. This fine impression was a significant addition to the outstanding group of etchings by Jacques Bellange acquired in 1941 from the Robert-Dumesnil collection. The Raising of Lazarus was one of the many important gifts of the niece of W. G. Russell Allen in his memory. Mr. Allen generously helped the museum in many ways during his lifetime and left his superb collection of Goyas, Gauguins, and chiaroscuro prints, as well as a number of modern prints and illustrated books, as a bequest.

References: A. P. Robert-Dumesnil, *Le peintre-graveur français* (Paris, 1841–1871), vols. 5, 11, no. 6; Sue Welsh Reed, "The Etchings of Jacques Bellange," in *Prints,* ed. Carl Zigrosser (New York, 1962), pp. 131–154; Nicole Walch, *Die Radierungen des Jacques Bellange* (Munich, 1971).

76 *(photographed before restoration)*
BERNARDO STROZZI, Italian, 1581–1644
St. Sebastian
Oil on canvas; 167.4 × 118.5 cm.
Charles Potter Kling and Francis Welch Funds. 1972.83

With the purchase of Strozzi's **St. Sebastian,** *the museum acquired not only a painting of considerable distinction but one that filled two voids in the collection. The painting is the first work by the Genoese artist in the museum as well as in the Boston area, and, being of the master's Venetian period, it is illustrative of Venetian seventeenth-century painting hitherto unrepresented. Most significantly, it is related to the altarpiece for San Benedetto in Venice, generally considered with the* Rape of Europa *(Museo Nazionale, Poznan) as Strozzi's masterpieces. Compositional changes, principally involving the two attending women, St. Irene and her servant, and the reduction in size suggest that the Boston version was in all likelihood a study for the altarpiece, although evidence to the contrary may come to light with amplification of its provenance.*

77

GIUSEPPE MARIA CRESPI, Italian, 1665–1747
The Lute Player
Ca. 1700–1705; oil on canvas; 121.3 × 153 cm.
Charles Potter Kling Fund. 69.958

The emphasis placed on the musical instrument and the pensive mood of the lutenist suggest that the painting was intended to be an allegory of music. An eighteenth-century manuscript records a painting of a Donna che accorda il liuto, *belonging to a Signor Zanoli of Leghorn (MS. 131, c. 360, Biblioteca Comunale, Bologna), which Dwight Miller suggests more likely corresponds to the Boston Crespi than does reference by Giovanni Zanotti (*Storia dell'Accademia Clementina, Bologna, 1739, vol. 2, p. 64*) to two half-length figures representing music and sculpture. Yet another reference (MS. B 109, Pt. 2, p. 5) is cited by Mrs. M. P. Merriman, in an unpublished catalogue entry, to a painting of a woman playing a lute, a* mezzo figura grande come naturale quadro per traverso *in the home of Giacomo Marchesini, which she believes may apply to this exceptional Bolognese painting.*

References: Pittura del '600 Emiliano *(Bologna, 1959), pp. 202–203, no. 103;* Centennial Acquisitions, *special issue of* Boston Museum Bulletin *68 (1970), no. 49; Dwight Miller, "Bologna and Emilia," in* Painting in Italy in the 18th century: Rococo to Romanticism *(Chicago 1970), p. 116, no. 45.*

78

Giovanni Battista Tiepolo, Venetian, 1696–1770
Time Unveiling Truth
Ca. 1745; oil on canvas; 231.7 × 167.6 cm.
Charles Potter Kling Fund. 61.1200

One of the most magnificent rococo paintings in the United States and one of the largest easel paintings by Tiepolo, this rare picture brings together the artist's superb draftsmanship, remarkable brushwork, and soaring imagination. The earliest record of this painting comes with its purchase in Venice by Baron de Schwiter of Paris in 1865. The Venetian court refused export of the picture owing to its importance, but at the time of Austria's cession of Venice to Italy, two years later, the painting was removed to Vienna by diplomatic pouch and then to Baron Schwiter in Paris, later passing to the Blumenthal Collection, Paris.

References: Antonio Morassi, *Tiepolo* (Bergamo, 1943), p. 26; Giulo Lorenzetti, *Mostra del Tiepolo* (Venice, 1951), p. 84, no. 62.; Perry T. Rathbone in *Museum of Fine Arts, Boston: Western Art* (Boston, 1971), no. 100.

100

79

JOSEPH EFFNER (designer), German, 1687–1745
Console table
1720–1740; gilt oak, marble top; h. 85.6 cm., w. 1.5 m., d. 64.5 cm.
Helen and Alice Colburn Fund. 57.658

The rich but controlled display of ornament applied to this splendid console table, the arms of Austria crowning the stretcher, and the emblazoned medallion portrait evoke the glitter, elegance, and liveliness of the German rokoko, which flourished in court centers such as Munich, Nymphenburg, and Schleissheim in the first half of the eighteenth century. Our table is one of a pair; the other, which bears a male portrait and the arms of Bavaria, is in Frankfurt. Both are attributable to the court architect Joseph Effner, and the portraits are thought to be those of the Elector Karl Albert of Bavaria (the Frankfurt table) and his wife Maria Amalie, daughter of the Emperor Charles VI (the Boston table). The table represents, beyond its inherent beauty, a synthesis of the eighteenth-century south German court taste under strong French influence.

References: Hanns Swarzenski in *Museum of Fine Arts, Boston: Western Art* (Boston, 1971), no. 48; R. and H. Jedding, *Der Konsoltisch im Werk Joseph Effners* (Munich, 1960), pp. 231–248.

101

80

Monkey holding a snuff box

Germany (Meissen), ca. 1730; luster painted porcelain; h. 48.2 cm., w. 19 cm., d. 22.5 cm.
William F. Warden Fund. 58.1190

Modeled either by J. G. Kirchner or J. J. Kaendler, both master modelers of the Meissen
porcelain factory, the monkey is also distinguished by the mark "AR," identifying it as a
commission for Augustus the Strong, major force and great patron of the factory. The
superb modeling of this droll beast and the rendering of the gesture represent the
highest achievement of the Meissen works, which first discovered, in the west, and did
much to develop the technique of hard-paste porcelain work. The model was produced
by the factory in a number of contemporary and later variations. The very large number
of these derivative variations of the model, both at Meissen and other factories, cannot
be explained merely by the fact that monkeys were favorite pets of eighteenth-century
society. The creature was also regarded as a satirical symbol of human vanity and
foibles.

Reference: Hanns Swarzenski in *Museum of Fine Arts, Boston: Western Art* (Boston 1971),
no. 59.

102

81

Soup tureen and stand

Germany (Meissen), ca. 1740–45; porcelain; tureen: h. 21.9 cm., l. 31.1 cm., w. 26.7 cm.; stand: l. 39.4 cm., w. 28.4 cm.

Bequest of Forsyth Wickes; Forsyth Wickes Collection. 65.2072

This superb tureen features a boar's head finial, set amongst large colorful scrolls in shell form. The device, drawn from contemporary French goldsmith work, was often used on other tureens produced at the Meissen factory. The military and camp scenes are taken from Augsburg prints. They allude to the wars between Austria and the Turks in 1739 and 1740. The polychrome flowers, derived from engravings by J. S. Weinman, are painted on a white ground, bringing a necessary levity to the work. Shaded gilt trellis and scroll work frame the reserves. These, together with the gilded shell-shaped handles, give to the piece a full measure of the rococo spirit.

Collection: Alfred Horstmann, Berlin.

References: Metropolitan Museum of Art, New York, *European Porcelain Exhibition* (New York, 1949), no. 326; Carl Dauterman, "Porcelain in the Forsyth Wickes Collection," *Antiques,* October 1968, 348; Perry T. Rathbone, *The Forsyth Wickes Collection,* Museum of Fine Arts, Boston (Boston, 1968), p. 34.

82

JACQUES VAN OOSTENRYK (DAUTRICHE), French, died 1778
Commode
Ca. 1760; pallisandre and fruit woods, marquetry, ormolu mounts; h. 87.7 cm.,
w. 1.26 m., d. 57.2 cm.
Gift of Jack Linsky. 67.1192

*On becoming a master cabinetmaker in 1765, Jacques Dautriche was notably proficient
in marquetry work. In this Louis XVI commode, stamped "Dautriche," the execution
of marquetry is a great achievement in design and technique. The vertical diaper pattern
on the three sides is expertly complimented by the horizontal ormolu guilloche pattern
in openwork. The ormolu plaques on the center and the apron depict classical subjects:
sacrifice of Cupid (possibly a Clodion invention) and Medusa.*

Collection: Oskar Bondy, Vienna.

83

PIERRE MACRET, French, 1726–1796
Lady's writing desk (bureau de dame)
Paris, ca. 1760; veneered red, gold, and black lacquer, ormolu mounts; h. 82.5 cm.,
w. 83.2 cm., d. 43.2 cm.
Bequest of Forsyth Wickes; Forsyth Wickes Collection. 65.2506

The bureau de dame is an exquisite work of art, employing the eighteenth-century taste
for lacquer work. The oriental influence, with the gilded chinoiserie decoration against
a red background, combines easily with the western influence of the slightly bombé and
cabriole style of the body and legs. The cavetto-shaped drop front opens to a tulipwood
interior, exposing six drawers, a secret niche, and a gold-tooled, green leather writing
surface – all executed with a delicateness and an appropriateness to the individual's use.

Collection: A. Fauchier Magnan, Paris.

References: Perry T. Rathbone, *The Forsyth Wickes Collection,* Museum of Fine Arts, Boston
(Boston, 1968), pp. 43–44; Hanns Swarzenski in *Museum of Fine Arts, Boston: Western Art*
(Boston, 1971), no. 51.

84

Soup tureen and stand

France (Vincennes), 1756; porcelain; tureen: h. 29.7 cm., d. 22.8 cm.; stand: l. 45.5 cm., w. 36.6 cm.

Bequest of Forsyth Wickes; Forsyth Wickes Collection. 65.1885

Jean-Claude Duplessis, royal goldsmith, was commissioned by Louis XV to be responsible for the forms and modeled decoration at the Vincennes-Sèvres factory. Accepting this charge, he was able to successfully translate silver models into the new soft-paste medium. This ability is quite apparent in the design of this tureen. Feet in the form of celery stalks and the naturalistically rendered orange finial are skillfully modeled. The gold-bordered reserve panels, depicting cupids in the manner of François Boucher, birds, flowers, and emblems of music and the hunt, are painted probably by Dodin and other decorators. This tureen comes from a service ordered by Catherine II of Russia. Three other related tureens are at the Campbell Museum, Camden, New Jersey; The Metropolitan Museum of Art, New York; and the Museum of Cleveland, Ohio.

References: John C. Austin, *The Campbell Museum Collection* (Camden, 1969), no. 40; Perry T. Rathbone, *The Forsyth Wickes Collection,* Museum of Fine Arts, Boston (Boston, 1968), p. 28; Hanns Swarzenski in *Museum of Fine Arts, Boston: Western Art* (Boston, 1971), no. 57.

85

JEAN ANTOINE WATTEAU, French, 1684–1721
Four studies of a woman
Ca. 1716–1717; trois crayons (sanguine, white, and black chalk) on tan paper;
34.1×24.1 cm.
Bequest of Forsyth Wickes; Forsyth Wickes Collection. 65.2610

The Forsyth Wickes bequest includes an impressive group of over seventy eighteenth-century drawings. This Watteau sheet of studies is one of the most typical of the French rococo era, with its delicate handling of the three colors of chalk and the subtle placement of the figures on the paper.

Watteau filled many volumes with sketches and studies, and from these he drew inspiration for his paintings. The woman in the upper left appears in two paintings:
The Game of Love *(National Gallery, London), and* Assembly in a Park *(formerly in the Kaiser Friedrich collection). Watteau seems to have made two counterproofs of this drawing, one of which is in the British Museum.*

References: Wendy T. Topkins in *Museum of Fine Arts, Boston: Western Art* (Boston, 1971),
no. 131; K. T. Parker and J. Mathey, *Antoine Watteau: Catalogue complet de son œuvre dessiné*
(Paris, 1957), vol. 2, no. 786; Perry T. Rathbone, *The Forsyth Wickes Collection*, Museum of
Fine Arts, Boston (Boston, 1968), pp. 12–14.

86

GABRIEL DE SAINT-AUBIN, French, 1724–1780

Lully's opera Armide *performed at the Palais-Royal*

Probably 1761; pen, watercolor, and gouache over pencil; 31.1 × 50.2 cm.

Centennial Gift of Elizabeth Paine Card in memory of her father, Robert Treat Paine II.
1970.36

This Saint-Aubin drawing of an operatic performance was acquired by the Hermitage before 1797 but was sold in 1932, when the Soviet government was raising money. An old inscription in French on the Hermitage mount identifies the opera as Armide *and the theater as the old* salle de l'opéra, *painted by Saint-Aubin in 1747. Dacier states in his catalogue raisonné of Saint-Aubin's drawings that he could find no record of a performance of Lully's* Armide *in 1747, but that it was given a lavish production in this little theater in the Palais-Royal in 1761. Dacier believes that the drawing was done at that time. The theater was destroyed by fire in 1763 before any subsequent production of the opera.*

Reference: Émile Dacier, *Gabriel de Saint-Aubin* (Paris, 1931), vol. 2, no. 745.

108

87

JOHAN (or FRANZ) MARTIN MUTSCHELE, German, 1733–1804
Madonna of Victory (from Wolfram-Eschenbach)
Signed J. M. M. and dated 1771; Schrezheim faience; h. 1.23 m., w. 38 cm., d. 29.5 cm.
William F. Warden Fund. 61.1185

*This shimmering vision of the Madonna, the Madonna of Victory, finds its thematic
source in Revelation 12: "And there appeared a great wonder in heaven, a woman
clothed with the sun and the moon under her feet and upon her head a crown of twelve
stars." Every line, every form, every part of the surface vibrates a spiritual energy. Originally commissioned from Mutschele for placement under a canopy in a niche over a
doorway, the figure is a summary of South German rococo and the acknowledged masterpiece of eighteenth-century German faience sculpture.*

References: S. Ducret, *German Porcelain and Faience* (New York, 1962), p. 435 f., no. 176; Hanns
Swarzenski, "A Frankish Faience Madonna," Museum of Fine Arts, *Bulletin* 63 (1965), 183–198;
Hanns Swarzenski in *Museum of Fine Arts, Boston: Western Art* (Boston, 1971), no. 60.

88

St. John

Austria, ca. 1740; polychromed limewood;
h. 1.83 m., w. 61 cm., d. 58.4 cm.
William F. Warden Fund. 1972.46

*Like the fourteenth-century St. John in this ex-
hibition (see no. 52), this figure is apparently the
only one to survive from a group which may have
depicted the swooning, mourning Virgin supported and comforted by St. John. That St. John's
glance is directed downward, and that the figure
appears to rotate around a vertical axis, supports
this view. The virtuoso quality of the carving is
apparent not only in the sense of the movement
conveyed despite the fragmentary state but also in
the rippling drapery, so descriptive of the body beneath, the elegant line of the clothing at the throat,
the flickering forms of the hair, the sensitivity of
the expression. The figure is an extraordinary,
isolated work of an as yet unknown master.*

89

SEBASTIEN BOURDON, French, 1616–1671
Rebecca and Eliezar (not illustrated)
Christ and the Woman of Samaria
After 1658; oil on canvas; each 144.8×200.5 cm.
Robert J. Edwards Fund. 68.23, 68.24

Bourdon seems to have treated the Old Testament story (Genesis 24: 10–28) three other times. One painting is mentioned in the Duke of Portland's collection in 1938 (Burlington Magazine, 72, February 1938, 62). Two are mentioned by C. Ponsonailhe (Sebastien Bourdon, Paris, 1883, pp. 297, 309). The pairing of that story with another instance of a revelation at a well drawn from the New Testament is unusual; thus, these are a significant addition to the museum's seventeenth-century French collection. It is also noteworthy that they are documented in the seventeenth-century as having been commissioned by an Abbé de Saint-Georges after Bourdon's last trip to Montpellier in 1658. Geraldine Fowle, of the University of Missouri-Kansas City, has located mention of the pair in the 1777 sale catalogue of the collection of the Prince de Conti.

References: Guillet de St. Georges, "Mémoire historique des principaux ouvrages de M. Bourdon," in Ph. de Chennevieres et al., *Mémoires inedits sur la vie et les ouvrages de l'Academie Royale de Peinture et de Sculpture* (Paris, 1854), vol. 1, p. 94, inventory of June 7, 1692; *Centennial Acquisitions*, special issue of *Boston Museum Bulletin* 68 (1970), 76–77, nos. 47, 48.

90

Nicolas Lancret, French, 1690–1745
Le Déjeuner de jambon
Ca. 1735; oil on canvas; 56.4 × 46.7 cm.
Bequest of Forsyth Wickes; Forsyth Wickes Collection. 65.2649

*The most important of twenty paintings presented with the Wickes bequest to the
museum in 1965 is this delightfully uninhibited scene of feasting. It is an original study
for the larger composition painted in 1735 by order of Louis XV, appropriately for the
dining room of the* petits appartements *at Versailles. The larger version and its pendant,*
Le Déjeuner d'huitres *by Jean-Francois de Troy (1679–1752), survive in the Musée Condé
in Chantilly. Except for the noticeable addition of an overturned chair in the lower
right corner and the substitution of a statue of Bacchus atop the pedestal for a huge
marble vase, the Chantilly painting is identical to the smaller oil, which was engraved
in 1756 by Pierre Étienne Moitte (1722–1780) and dedicated to the Marquis de la Live de
Jully, in whose collection the painting was catalogued in 1764.*

References: Georges Wildenstein, *Lancret* (Paris, 1924), no. 74; Gabriel Henroit, *Collection
David-Weill: Peintures* (Paris, 1926), vol. 1, pt. 2, pp. 223–225; Perry T. Rathbone, *The Forsyth
Wickes Collection, Museum of Fine Arts, Boston* (Boston, 1968), pp. 18, 19.

112

91

FRANS HALS, Dutch, 1580–1666
Portrait of a Man
Ca. 1664–1666; oil on canvas; 85 × 66.7 cm.
Gift of Mrs. Antonie Lilienfeld in memory of Dr. Leon Lilienfeld. 66.1054

Characteristic of the artist's late expressive brushwork and similar in pose to other portraits of the 1660's, the Lilienfeld Hals portrays a sitter whose identity is unknown. The excessive length of the gentleman's hair, as Seymour Slive points out, is indicative of the penchant in Holland at that time for the fashions of Louis XIV, which also caused a change in tonality in the artist's late paintings. Of singular distinction, the Portrait of a Man *joins Rembrandt's* Elison *portraits, Ruisdael's* Rough Sea, *Aert de Gelder's* Rest on the Flight into Egypt, *and Ter Borch's* Cavalier in the Saddle, *all acquired since 1955 to strengthen the Dutch seventeenth-century painting collection.*

References: Gustav Glück, *Niederländische Gemälde aus der Sammlung des Herrn Dr. Leon Lilienfeld in Wien* (Vienna, 1917), pp. 54 f., 63, no. 25, repr. as frontis.; *Centennial Acquisitions,* special issue of *Boston Museum Bulletin* 68 (1970), 80, no. 50; Seymour Slive, *Frans Hals* (London, 1970), vol. 1, p. 208; vol 2, pl. 337.

92

REMBRANDT VAN RIJN, Dutch, 1606–1669

Reverend Johannes Elison
1634; oil on canvas; 174 × 173 cm.
William K. Richardson Fund. 56.510

Mevr. Johannes Elison (Maria Bockenolle)
1634; oil on canvas; 174.5 × 124 cm.
William K. Richardson Fund. 56.511

The Elison's son Johannes, a prosperous businessman, commissioned these portraits of his parents, leaders of the Dutch colony in Norwich, England. The choice of Rembrandt to do these portraits indicates the renown this young artist had already attained. The paintings, which are in extraordinarily good condition, are distinguished by their brilliant characterizations and the fact that they are one of two known pairs of full-length portraits by Rembrandt.

References: Jakob Rosenberg, "Rembrandt's Portraits of Johannes Elison and his Wife," Museum of Fine Arts, Boston, *Bulletin* 55 (1957), 3–9; Horst Gerson, *Rembrandt Paintings* (Amsterdam, 1968), p. 286, no. 162; Perry T. Rathbone in *Museum of Fine Arts, Boston: Western Art* (Boston, 1971), nos. 107, 139.

93

REMBRANDT VAN RIJN, Dutch, 1606–1669
Watchdog Sleeping in his Kennel
Ca. 1633; pen, bistre, and gallnut ink; 14.2 × 16.5 cm.
J. H. and E. A. Payne Fund. 56.519

The Watchdog Sleeping in his Kennel *is the first significant Rembrandt drawing acquired by the museum. It is a striking example of the artist's early style, in which lights and darks are strongly contrasted. The inks and washes blend and blur, yet the comfortable kennel and the animal's textured coat are clearly suggested. The curled up, sleeping dog observed in the 1637 painting of* Joseph Telling his Dreams *(Rijksmuseum, Amsterdam) and the one in the small etching* A Sleeping Puppy *(Hind 174), of 1640, are both closely related to the drawing.*

References: Otto Benesch, *The Drawings of Rembrandt* (London, 1954), no. 455, fig. 510; Rijksmuseum, Amsterdam, *Rembrandt, 1669–1969*, p. 118, no. 29; Christopher White, *Rembrandt as an Etcher: A Study of the Artist at Work* (London, 1969), pp. 159–160, 165, pl. 230.

116

94

GERARD TER BORCH, Dutch, 1584–1662
Cavalier in the Saddle
Oil on panel; 55 × 41 cm.
Robert J. Edwards Fund, Julia Cheney Edwards Collection. 61.660

An especially fine, very early Ter Borch, this panel is one of three versions. The other two are in a private collection in Holland, and in the collection of Mrs. M. A. Dunne, England (documented in S. J. Gudlaugsson, Ter Borch, The Hague, 1959, vol. 1, pp. 176, 177). The Boston panel was not known by Gudlaugsson until after 1959, but he has subsequently dated it between the other two on stylistic grounds. Several drawings of the same period are indicative of Ter Borch's fascination with the problems presented by his choice of subject matter. The painting's provenance has not been established prior to its ownership by Mrs. William R. Mercer (Martha Dana) of Doylstown, Pennsylvania, formerly of Boston.

95

JACOB VAN RUISDAEL, Dutch, 1628–1682
A Rough Sea
Ca. 1670; oil on canvas; 107 × 124.5 cm.
William F. Warden Fund. 57.4

Once in the Sir Otto Beit Collection in London, A Rough Sea shows a view of the estuary of the Ij River outside Amsterdam. Ruisdael, together with his fellow landscape painters of seventeenth-century Holland, chose a closeness to nature as the inspiration for their work. With understanding and keen observation of nature Ruisdael conveys the threatening yet beautiful effect of wind at sea.

References: Wolfgang Stechow, *Dutch Landscape Painting of the Seventeenth Century* (London, 1966), p. 122, pl. 247; Wilhelm Bode, *Catalogue of the Collection of Pictures and Bronzes in the Possession of Otto Beit* (London, 1913), p. 19 f., pl. XV; Perry T. Rathbone in *Museum of Fine Arts, Boston: Western Art* (Boston, 1971), no. 105.

118

96

Aert de Gelder, Dutch, 1645–1727
Rest on the Flight into Egypt
Ca. 1690; oil on canvas; 110 × 118 cm.
Maria T. B. Hopkins Fund. 57.182

This beautifully simple representation of the flight into Egypt demonstrates the concern in the seventeenth-century Protestant north with humanizing biblical scenes. Aert de Gelder studied with the elderly Rembrandt (1609–1669) and much of that artist's late manner can be seen in the vigorous brushwork, luminous color, and special effect of light in the Boston painting, which nonetheless displays Aert de Gelder's own interpretative qualities.

Reference: Kurt Lilienfeld, *Aert de Gelder* (The Hague, 1914), p. 148, no. 53.

97

GEORGE ROMNEY, British, 1734–1802

Anne, Lady de la Pole

1786; oil on canvas; 243 × 150 cm.

Given in memory of Governor Alvan T. Fuller by the Fuller Foundation. 61.392

A brilliant example of courtly eighteenth-century English portraiture, Romney's Lady Anne *has special significance for Boston, being perhaps the finest Romney in the United States as well as having come from the collection of the late Governor Alvan T. Fuller of Massachusetts. The full-length portrait of Anne and its companion piece of her husband, Sir John William de la Pole of Devonshire, now in the Wadsworth Athenaeum, Hartford, were painted in 1786, five years after their marriage. Sittings for the portraits are in fact recorded in Romney's diary in January, February and May 1786. Both paintings remained in the family until 1913.*

References: Humphry Ward and William Roberts, *Romney: A Biographical and Critical Essay* (New York, 1904), vol 2, p. 124 (erroneously listed as half-length portraits); Museum of Fine Arts, Boston, *Alvan T. Fuller Memorial Exhibition*, (Boston, 1959), p. 22, no. 27; Perry T. Rathbone in *Museum of Fine Arts, Boston: Western Art* (Boston, 1971), no. 140.

120

98

Box

England, 1650–1700; silk, metal, and seed pearls, embroidered; wax effigy inside cover;
h. 36 cm., w. 32 cm.

Gift of Mrs. Elizabeth Learned Peabody. 59.1033

*This jewelry casket has the story of Isaac and Rebecca (Genesis 24) as the main theme
of its embroidery, with other Old Testament scenes as well as various birds, animals,
insects, and flowers filling the remaining surfaces. The raised stumpwork figures
clothed in needlework have faces and hands of finely carved wood. The superb quality
of workmanship suggests that the casket was made by professional craftsmen.*

Collection: Dyson Perrins.

121

99

Bed furnishings and chair seat covers
England, 1675–1725; wool, linen, and cotton; embroidered.
Wide bed curtains: h. 216 cm., w. 264 cm.
Narrow bed curtains: h. 216 cm., w. 142 cm.
Two long pieces of valance: h. 33 cm., w. 189 cm., and h. 33 cm., w. 203 cm.
Short piece of valance: h. 33 cm., w. 132 cm.
Chair seat cover: front, w. 74 cm., back, w. 56 cm.; depth, 48 cm.
J. H. and E. A. Payne Fund. 63.1023–63.1029

*These embroideries constitute a nearly complete set of bedroom furnishings: two wide
and two narrow bed curtains, a valance in three pieces, and seven chair seat covers.
Bizarre flowers, exotic fruits and leaves extend from two different kinds of trees,
worked in yellow and red yarns with touches of orange and brown. The pattern is similar to that of laces, various silk weavings and Indian painted cottons of the late seventeenth and early eighteenth centuries.*

Reference: Lisa Cook Terrace, "English and New England Embroidery," Museum of Fine Arts,
Boston, *Bulletin* 62 (1964), 72–75, figs. 6, 7.

122

V EUROPEAN ART
19TH & 20TH CENTURIES

100

John Martin, English, 1789–1854
The Seventh Plague of Egypt
1823; oil on canvas; 145 × 214.5 cm.
Francis Welch Fund. 60.1157

When first shown early in 1824 at the inaugural exhibition of the Society of British Artists, Martin's painting interpreting Exodus 9: 23–25, was widely acclaimed. The same year, according to Balston, a sketch (probably in oil) for the painting was exhibited at the British Institution, and a mezzotint forming part of Martin's Illustrations of the Bible, *issued in 1835, made the painting even more popular. Characteristic of the British nineteenth-century romantic movement, the painting is of further interest because of Martin's early, although inaccurate, use of Egyptian motifs. One must assume that Martin was influenced by the first illustrated publications of Egyptian monuments, which were appearing at that time.*

Reference: Thomas Balston, *John Martin, His Life and Works* (London, 1947), pp. 78, 118, 249; Dows Dunham, "A Footnote to the History of Egyptology," American Research Center in Egypt, Inc., *Newsletter* 42 (July 1961), 3 ff.

124

101

<small>Francisco Goya y Lucientes</small>, Spanish, 1746–1828
The Giant (Colossus)
By 1818; aquatint (Delteil 35, first state); 28.6 × 20.9 cm.
Katherine Eliot Bullard Fund. 65.1296

As late as the earlier part of our century, Goya's prints were not, on the whole, highly regarded in Anglo-Saxon countries, because of his use of expressive rather than tidy techniques. The foundation of the museum's collection of prints by this artist goes back to 1894, when the museum bought its first etching by him. In 1951 the museum became one of the most important centers in the world for the study of Goya prints when it acquired eighty-eight trial proofs. Mr. Rathbone has furthered with enthusiasm the acquisition of this artist's graphic work. From 1955 to 1972 the Department of Prints and Drawings acquired a number of important Goyas, among them eleven drawings, two very rare lithographs, three double-sided copper plates, and the enigmatic Giant, *as superb as it is rare. One other impression of the first state is known, and no more than four of the second state.*

References: Loys Delteil, *Francisco Goya*, Le peintre graveur illustré, vol. 14 (Paris, 1922), no. 35; Tomás Harris, *Goya: Engravings and Lithographs* (Oxford, 1964), vol. 1, pp. 87, 89; vol. 2, no. 29; Eleanor A. Sayre in *Museum of Fine Arts, Boston: Western Art* (Boston, 1971), no. 146.

102

Francisco Goya y Lucientes, Spanish, 1746–1828
Reclining Nude
1825; watercolor and tempera on ivory; 88 × 86 cm.
Ernest Wadsworth Longfellow Fund. 63.1081

In a letter to his friend Joaquin Ferrer (Bordeaux, December 20, 1825), Goya wrote "It is true that last winter I painted on ivory, and I have a collection of some forty experiments, but it is a new kind of miniature which I never saw before, because it is not done with stippling–things which look more like the brushwork of Velazquez than of Mengs." Our miniature is very freely painted and has none of the tight, precise quality that is typical of miniature painting.

References: Martin Sebastian Soria, "Las Miniaturas y Retratos-Miniaturas de Goya," *Cobalto*, fasc. 2 (Barcelona, 1949), fig. 8; Eleanor A. Sayre, "Goya's Bordeaux Miniatures," *Boston Museum Bulletin* 64 (1966), 84 ff.

126

103

Edouard Manet, French, 1832–1883

Christ Mocked

Probably 1860–1865; pen and brown ink, brush and brown wash over pencil;
26.9 × 21.0 cm.

Arthur Tracy Cabot Fund and Centennial Gift of Mrs. Thomas Card and Anonymous
Donor. 68.755

The Christ Mocked *was acquired from the estate of Dr. Georg Swarzenski, who had
been Fellow for Research in Sculpture and Decorative Arts at this museum. The drawing
is a restatement by Manet in his own terms of Titian's great painting in the Louvre,*
Christ Crowned with Thorns; *Manet was engaged in a number of such exercises in the
early 1860's. The drawing seems to be the source of his painting of the same subject,
dated 1865, in the Art Institute of Chicago. There is a copy of this drawing in the
Wallraf-Richartz-Museum, Cologne.*

Reference: Curt Glaser, *Edouard Manet: Faksimiles nach Zeichnungen und Aquarellen*
(Munich, 1922), pl. V.

104

Edouard Manet, French, 1832–1883
La Leçon de musique
1870; oil on canvas; 140×173 cm.
Given in memory of Charles Deering. 69.1123

*In 1870 two paintings by Manet were accepted by the academically controlled Salon,
which had in inconsistent fashion rejected and accepted work by Manet and some of
his friends in previous years. Although Manet had participated in the Salon des Refusés
in 1863, he continued to attempt to exhibit his work in orthodox channels.* The Music
Lesson *(no. 1851) and Manet's portrait of Éva Gonzalès, who only the year before had
become his pupil, were exhibited. Evidently the Boston double portrait was received
with indifference by the public, but only fourteen years later it was included in the
memorial exhibition at the École des Beaux-Arts the year after Manet's death. As in the
case of* The Street Singer, *1862 (Museum of Fine Arts, Boston) and* The Balcony, *1869
(Louvre), Manet in* The Music Lesson *utilized acquaintances rather than professional
models. Zacharie Astruc, a close friend who is also shown with Manet and others in
Fantin-Latour's painting exhibited at the Salon the same year,* Un atelier aux Batig-
nolles, *is the guitarist. The singer's identity remains unknown, although an oil sketch
exists (Jamot, no. 176) and a small oil by Éva Gonzalès, dated 1869–70 and corrected
by Manet, seems to represent the same person (Art News, January 1971, p. 32).*

References: Paul Jamot and Georges Wildenstein, *Manet* (Paris, 1932), no. 177, fig. 168; *Centennial Acquisitions,* special issue of *Boston Museum Bulletin* 68 (1970) 87, no. 57.

128

105

EDGAR DEGAS, French, 1834–1917
Deux jeunes femmes visitant un musée
Ca. 1877–1880; oil on canvas; 90 × 67 cm.
Anonymous Gift. 69.49

The Deux jeunes femmes *belongs to a loosely knit series of oils, pastels, and prints
made by Degas from 1877 to 1880 of one woman, sometimes with a companion, in a
museum. A pastel of 1880 depicting Mary Cassatt in the Louvre accompanied by a
seated lady peering around her guidebook and another of the same date with the figures
rearranged (Lemoisne, 581, 583) have occasioned the theory because of their resemblance to the Boston oil, that Mary Cassatt is the figure on the left and the other her
sister, Lydia. Lemoisne, however, does not identify either woman or the single figure in
another oil closely related to the Boston oil (Lemoisne, 464, 465). Two sketches for the
1880 pastel (Lemoisne, 582; 3ème Vente Degas, no. 150) and two etchings (Deteil, 29,
30) further indicate Degas' preoccupation with the theme.*

References: Galerie Georges Petit, *Catalogue des tableaux, pastels, et dessins par Edgar Degas et
provenant de son atelier,* 1e Vente, May 6–8, 1918, no. 34; Paul A. Lemoisne, *Degas et son œuvre*
(Paris, 1946), vol. 2, no. 464; *Centennial Acquisitions,* special issue of *Boston Museum Bulletin* 68
(1970), 90, no. 58, and cover.

106

EDGAR DEGAS, French, 1834–1917

a. *La Sieste (Scène de maison close)*
Monotype in black ink; plate: 21.5 × 16.0 cm.
Katherine Eliot Bullard Fund. 61.1215

b. *Le Cabinet particulier*
Monotype in black ink; plate: 16.0 × 21.5 cm.
Katherine Eliot Bullard Fund. 61.1212

These monotypes are from a group of five, which the museum acquired in 1961. The monotype process permitted Degas to "draw" with printer's ink on a clean plate in a spontaneous and expressive way. No more than one or two impressions could be printed; Degas often used the second impression as a monotype base for his compositions in other media. Two superb pastel over monotype landscapes given to the museum by Denman Ross in 1909 are fine examples of Degas' skillful use of this uncommon technique.

Reference: Eugenia Parry Janis, *Degas Monotypes* (Cambridge, Mass., 1968), nos. 20, 28.

107 *(on loan in Munich to Olympic Games Exhibition, World Cultures and Modern Art)*
CLAUDE MONET, French, 1840–1926
La Japonaise
1876; oil on canvas; 231 × 142 cm.
1951 Purchase Fund. 56.147

In this painting Monet poses his first wife, Camille, like a giant Japanese print against a wall scattered with Japanese fans. La Japonaise *is the last major figure picture done by Monet. It was shown in the second Impressionist Exhibition at the Durand-Ruel galleries in 1876.*

References: Douglas Cooper, *Claude Monet* (London, 1957), p. 48; William Seitz, *Claude Monet* (New York, 1960), p. 104; Perry T. Rathbone in *Museum of Fine Arts, Boston: Western Art* (Boston, 1971), no. 116.

108

PAUL GAUGUIN, French, 1843–1903

"Soyez amoureuses vous serez heureuses"

Pont-Aven, Brittany, ca. 1889; carved and polychromed lindenwood; h. 1.20 m., w. 96 cm. (with original frame), d. 8 cm.

Arthur Tracy Cabot Fund. 57.582

In 1889 Gauguin wrote to Emile Bernard about this relief: "the best and strangest thing I have ever done in sculpture . . . Gauguin (like a monster)taking the hand of a woman who resists and telling her: 'Be in love and you'll be happy.' The fox is the Indian symbol for perversity and in the interstices are several small figures."

Like an image from a disturbing dream the relief weaves together currents of anxiety, suffering, and passion, which colored both Gauguin's life and his art. The richness of imagery is equaled by that of the relief's surface, where variegation of form, texture, and applied color have an exotic quality that prefigures Gauguin's later Tahitian works.

Reference: Hanns Swarzenski in *Museum of Fine Arts, Boston: Western Art* (Boston, 1971), no. 47.

132

109

Vincent Van Gogh, Dutch, 1853–1890
Young Girl
Charcoal and graphite, brown and black wash, heightened with white; 48.5 × 25.5 cm.
William Francis Warden Fund. 1970.468

*In December 1881 Van Gogh traveled to the Hague to seek advice of the painter Anton Mauve (1838–1888). By January of the following year Van Gogh wrote in a letter to his brother: "But, Theo, I can assure you that when I went to Mauve for the first time with my pen drawing and Mauve said, 'You must try it now with charcoal and crayon and brush and stump,' I had a deuced lot of trouble working with that new material. I was patient and it did not seem to help; then at times I became so impatient that I stamped on the charcoal and was utterly discouraged." (*The Complete Letters of Vincent Van Gogh, Greenwich, Conn.: New York Graphic Society [1958], vol. 1, p. 302).*

In this drawing, done in the early 1880's, Van Gogh has given the childish figure strength and dignity by bold delineation of form: rubbing, scraping, and gouging the surface of the tough, wove paper.

References: Jacob-Baart de la Faille, L'œuvre de Vincent Van Gogh: catalogue raisonné (Paris, and Brussels, 1928), vols. 3, 4; The Complete Letters of Vincent Van Gogh, 3 vols. (Greenwich, Conn. [1958]).

133

110

EDVARD MUNCH, Norwegian, 1863–1944
The Voice
1893; oil on canvas; 87.5 × 108 cm.
Ernest Wadsworth Longfellow Fund. 59.301

This early Munch is one of the few and probably the finest of the paintings by this artist in America, for which Dagny Juell served as the model. Her sister, Mrs. Rägnhild Bäckström of Stockholm, a close friend of the artist, was the original owner of the painting. A second version, ca. 1893, in the Munchmuseet, Oslo, and other works of the 1980's and early 1900's illustrate Munch's concern with some of the same symbolic elements that emphasize a sense of isolation and anxiety. A drypoint and aquatint of 1895 entitled Summernight *is a variation of* The Voice, *and a later woodcut of the same title contains the painting's central portion.*

References: Arve Moen, *Edvard Munch: Graphic Art and Paintings,* vol. 2, *Woman and Eros* (Oslo, 1957), pp. 18–20; Perry T. Rathbone in *Museum of Fine Arts, Boston: Western Art* (Boston, 1971), no. 120.

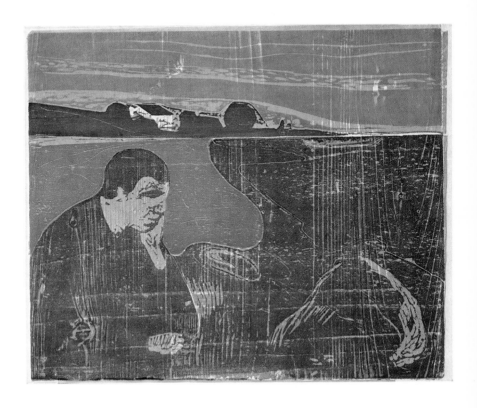

111

Edvard Munch, Norwegian, 1863–1944
Melancholy
1896; woodcut, printed in color; 37.6×45.5 cm.
William Francis Warden Fund. 57.356

Melancholy (*other titles are* Evening *and* On the Beach) *is one of a collection of Munch prints acquired in 1957. Edward Munch's early woodcuts influenced the style and expressive content of many of the finest twentieth-century woodcuts. His use of the natural grain of the blocks in which the design is cut was particularly influential. Like many of Munch's early woodcuts,* Melancholy *was printed in a number of subtly varied color combinations.*

Reference: Gustav Schiefler, *Verzeichnis des graphischen Werks Edvard Munchs, bis 1906* (Berlin, 1907), p. 77, no. 82 b.

112

Odilon Redon, French, 1840–1916
Centaur
Ca. 1895–1900; pastel on canvas; 73 × 61 cm.
Gift of Laurence K. Marshall. 64.2206

The Centaur *significantly represents Redon's highly imaginative use of supernatural and mythological themes. Stimulated by Darwin's theories, the artist produced a lithographic series* Les Origines *in 1883 in which a centaur appears. And there were earlier precedents; a drawing, for example, dated 1880–1889 (S. Sandström, Le Monde imaginaire d'Odilon Redon, Lund, 1955, fig 63, p. 82) depicting a battling centaur and centauress with bow and arrow, bears some resemblance to the Boston pastel. It was not until shortly before 1900 that Redon began to work in color in pastel.*

References: Klaus Berger, *Odilon Redon: Phantasie und Farbe* (Cologne, 1964), p. 207, no. 344; *Centennial Acquisitions,* special issue of the *Boston Museum Bulletin* 68 (1970), no. 88.

136

113

Oskar Kokoschka, Austrian, born 1886
Self-Portrait as a Warrior
1908; polychromed clay; h. 36.5 cm, w. 31.5 cm, d. 19.5 cm.
J. H. and E. A. Payne Fund. 60.958

In this head the Expressionist Kokoschka distorts his own features, distresses and disrupts natural form, and attacks the surface with disturbing oranges, blues, and yellows. The result is a jarring statement of the pain, agony, and, it seems, horror, which the artist feels and man can feel. The head appears to recoil from that which causes the emotion, thereby intensifying the expression of that emotion.

To the spectator attending the first Vienna Kunstschau in 1908, where the work was first exhibited, the Warrior *produced mostly indignation or ridicule. The artistic significance of the piece, however, was not lost upon the architect Adolf Loos, who acquired it immediately after the unsuccessful exhibition.*

References: H. M. Wingler, *Kokoschka* (Salzburg, 1956), p. 337; Hanns Swarzenski, "Recent Acquisitions of Contemporary Sculpture," Museum of Fine Arts, Boston, *Bulletin* 61 (1963), 94; Hanns Swarzenski in *Museum of Fine Arts, Boston: Western Art* (Boston, 1971), no. 61; Oskar Kokoschka, *Mein Leben* (Munich, 1969), p. 55.

114
PABLO PICASSO, Spanish, born 1881
Standing Figure
1908; oil on canvas; 149.8 × 100.4 cm.
Robert Jacob Edwards Fund. 59.976

This painting is one of a series of studies, and in particular of the central figure, for the Three Women *in the Hermitage in Leningrad. This picture was the first Picasso to come to the museum, providing a vital illustration of this period in the artist's development toward analytical cubism.*

Reference: Christian Zervos, *Pablo Picasso* (Paris, 1942), vol. 2, no. 103.

115

Ernst Ludwig Kirchner, German, 1880–1938
Reclining Nude
1909; oil on canvas; 74.5 × 151 cm.
Arthur Gordon Tompkins Residuary Fund. 57.2

The second painting by Kirchner to come into the museum's collection, the Reclining
Nude *is an early example of this great leader of the movement* Die Brücke. *Impatient
with the academic and with Impressionism, Kirchner began this movement in revolt,
as he said, to "revitalize German art and form a bridge through painting between art
and life."*

References: Museum of Fine Arts, Boston, *Bulletin* 58 (1960), 101; Donald Gordon, *Kirchner,*
(1968), no. 55, pl. 17.

116

Henri Gaudier-Brzeska, French, 1891–1915
The Wrestlers
1914; plaster relief; h. 71.8 cm., w. 92.1 cm.
Otis Norcross Fund. 65.1683

Gaudier-Brzeska's Wrestlers *expresses little of the application of force, much more of the artist's fascination with interwoven straplike forms, with constantly changing surface and volume, and sensitive use of line. The intensity of the image derives from the peculiar orchestration of form and line, not from the activity of the figures. The complexity of the poses suggests an encounter which will never end.*

A prodigy who took up the chisel only four years before his death, Gaudier-Brzeska was, because of his aggressive, imaginative approach to sculptural form, influential upon artists such as Henry Moore. A preliminary drawing for the relief is in the Department of Prints and Drawings. A canvas in oil, Portrait *of a Jew, was removed from the back of the relief and is now in the Department of Paintings.*

Reference: Jerome Peignot, Connaissance des arts, *May 1965, 65 ff.*

140

117
GASTON LACHAISE, French (born American), 1882–1935
Head of a woman
1923; polychromed mottled marble; h. 27.3 cm.
Gift of Margarett Sargent McKean in memory of Nathaniel Saltonstall. 68.789

*Lachaise, amateur of the female figure, focuses his interest upon the head of a lovely,
anonymous woman. The sensuousness that radiates from his figure studies is projected
here by the combination of curved, simplified forms and smooth surfaces. Still, this
head, as are the figures, is clothed with a certain remoteness. There exists also a version
in bronze, cast in 1962, last recorded in the estate of Isabel Lachaise (G. Nordland,
Lachaise, [Los Angeles, 1964], no. 38).*

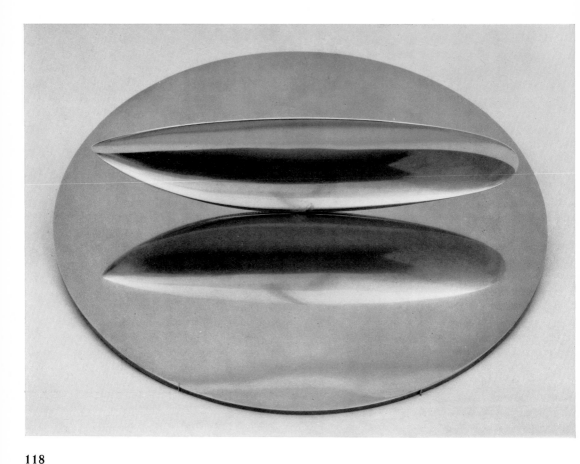

118

Constantin Brancusi, Roumanian, 1876–1957
The Golden Fish
1924; polished brass and steel; fish: h. 12.7 cm., l. 41.9 cm., d. 3 cm.; base: diam. 50 cm.
William F. Warden Fund. 57.739

Brancusi's Golden Fish begins its aesthetic statement by evoking through its stream-lined tapered shape the title image; the strength of the statement, however, lies in Brancusi's discovery and projection of essential form. In his use of carefully polished surfaces and a mirrored steel base, the artist envelopes this severely disciplined, cal-culated essay in a soft atmosphere of its own, indicating his profound sensitivity to the effect of light as well as form.

References: Hanns Swarzenski, "Recent Acquisitions of Contemporary Sculpture," Museum of Fine Arts, Boston, *Bulletin* 61 (1963), 91; Sidney Geist, *Brancusi, A Study of the Sculpture* (New York, 1968), no. 168 d; Solomon R. Guggenheim Museum, *Constantin Brancusi, 1876–1957, Retrospective Exhibition* (New York, 1969), p. 121; Hanns Swarzenski in *Museum of Fine Arts, Boston: Western Art* (Boston, 1971), no. 62.

119

EMIL NOLDE, German, 1867–1956

Iris

Watercolor; 47.0 × 34.3 cm.; signed lower right in gray wash: "Nolde"

Seth K. Sweetser Fund. 57.667

In 1927 Emil Nolde built a studio home at Seebüll in the isolated northern regions of Germany. His garden there became a constant source of imagery for him. Nolde's love of flowers is manifest in countless, vibrant watercolors. The Iris *is closely examined not for its botanical structure but for its brilliance of color, as contrasted with its essential delicacy and frailty. The museum owns two other watercolors by Nolde.*

Reference: Museum of Fine Arts, Boston, *European Masters of Our Time* (Boston, 1957), no. 111, fig. 89.

120

Juan Gris, Spanish, 1887–1927
Still Life with Guitar
1925; oil on canvas; 72.5 × 91.5 cm.
Gift of Joseph Pulitzer, Jr. 67.1161

With the gift of this late still life, the museum acquired its single example of Gris' work. Although not an innovator, Gris was a major contributor to the Cubist movement. His last paintings still demonstrate his capacity to use sensitively the Cubist language, which by the 1920's had nearly run its course.

References: Centennial Acquisitions, special issue of *Boston Museum Bulletin* 68 (1970), 138, no. 99; Charles S. Chetham et al., *Modern Paintings, Drawings, Sculpture Collected by Louise and Joseph Pulitzer, Jr.* (Cambridge, Mass., 1971), vol. 3, pp. 435–437, no. 179.

144

121

PAUL KLEE, Swiss, 1879–1940
Tanzt Entsetzen (He Dances Fright)
1931; pen and brown and reddish inks; 51 × 31.4 cm.
Gift of Mr. and Mrs. Richard K. Weil. 59.574

Tanzt Entsetzen *is one of six fine Klee drawings and watercolors acquired by the museum in recent years. Like many Klee works of the late twenties and early thirties, it explores the expressive possibilities of an image formed from a single continuous line. Here the line varies little in thickness but changes color as it "dances."*

145

122

MAX BECKMANN, German, 1884–1950

The Tempest

1947–1949; oil on paper on composition board; 180.5 × 65 cm.

Gift of Mrs. Max Beckmann. 58.24

Known originally as Jupiter, *the painting was begun in Holland in 1947, as recorded in Beckmann's* Tagebücher, 1904–1950 *(Munich, 1955), pp. 200, 202, and reconsidered in the spring of 1949 in St. Louis. At the urging of friends, Mr. Rathbone among them, Beckmann accepted in the fall of 1947 an appointment as professor of painting at the School of Fine Arts at Washington University in St. Louis. Beckmann there altered the painting's autobiographical basis, retitled it* The Tempest, *and inscribed it "St. L. 49." The precise meaning of the circular motif with fish and the two animal-headed trumpeting creatures above remains open to interpretation, but it is clear that "while the sheer, sensous pleasure of manipulating paint and color is the consuming passion of Beckmann's life, he never allows us to forget that first of all he is a humanist, whose brooding, introspective mind is concerned with man's emotions and man's experiences" (Perry T. Rathbone,* Max Beckmann, *St. Louis, 1948, p. 39).*

Reference: Hans M. F. von Erffa and Erhard Göpel, Blick auf Beckmann: Dokumente und Vorträge *(Munich, 1962), pp. 8, 255–256.*

146

123

MAX BECKMANN, German, 1884–1950
Shrimp Fisherman
1945; watercolor; 51.0×37.5 cm.
Abraham Shuman Fund. 68.58

*The serene yet brooding treatment of man and nature as seen in the unusual water-
color* Shrimp Fisherman *by Max Beckmann is unlike the German Expressionist's usual
highly charged, dramatic oil paintings filled with personal symbolism. Beckmann
had a great affection for the coast of Holland where he had fled in 1937. While
his watercolor is simple and direct, with no social commentary, it shares with his most
ambitious paintings the same expressive use of color and forceful structure.*

124

GIORGIO MORANDI, Italian, 1890–1964
Still Life
1946; oil on canvas; 25 × 45 cm.
Arthur Gordon Tompkins Residuary Fund. 61.662

One of a number of still lifes of similar composition, the museum's example shows that Morandi had established himself as one of the masters of still life painting of the twentieth century. This is the only painting by Morandi in the collection.

References: Cesare-Gnudi, *Morandi* (Florence, 1964), p. 64, no. 49; Daniel Robbins, "Recent Still-Life," *Art in America*, 1966, p. 57.

125

PABLO PICASSO, Spanish, born 1881

Plat blanc au poisson vert

Signed and dated 4. 4. 57; rose clay coated with pipe clay slip (engobe), partly glazed; diam. 44.8 cm., d. 5.7 cm.

Promised Gift of R. Thornton Wilson. 266.67

Simple, witty, direct, and typical of much of Picasso's later work, this charming nature morte pretends to nothing else than to express the artist's own amusement at his idea and his delight in the material with which he executes this idea. Working at Vallauris, near Cannes, France, Picasso began with a freshly turned plate, conjured a fish as only he can, and laid it forever on the plate – a generous serving of humor, texture, and color.

126 *(see overleaf)*

PABLO PICASSO, Spanish, born 1881

a. *Le Taureau*

1945; lithograph; third state of eleven; 33.6 × 51.6 cm. (sheet uneven)

Lee M. Friedman Fund. 1970.272

149

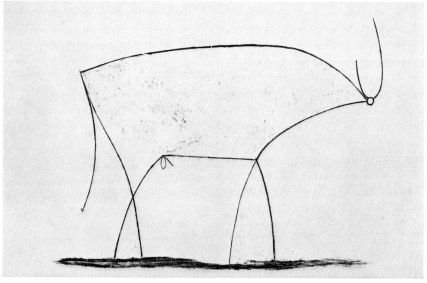

b. *Le Taureau*
1946; lithograph; eleventh and final state; 33.5 × 53.9 cm.
Lee M. Friedman Fund. 1970.277

In 1970 the museum acquired six of the eleven states of Picasso's lithograph of a bull, on which he worked from December 5, 1945, to January 7, 1946. What makes these proofs extraordinary is that they demonstrate the process by which a great artist has worked out his image by redrawing, scraping, and erasing. Picasso's final solution is a spare abstraction that conjures up a mere memory of the bull. Not only has he varied the treatment of the subject and the handling but he has also used papers that differ in character.

References: Fernand Mourlot, *Picasso Lithographe* (Monte-Carlo, 1949), vol. 1, no. 17, pp. 77–83 (all states illustrated); Museum of Fine Arts, Boston, *The Museum Year: 1969–70* (Boston, 1970), 53, 55.

150

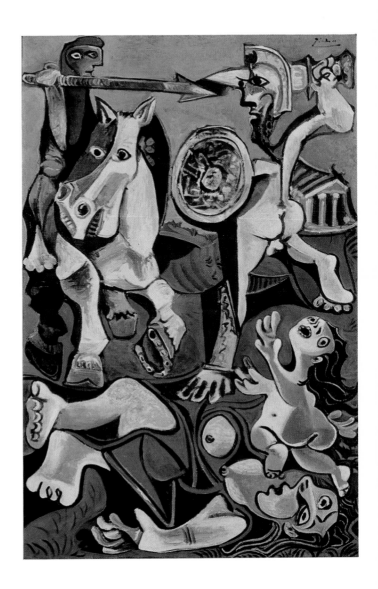

127

PABLO PICASSO, Spanish, born 1881
The Sabines
1963; oil on canvas; 195 × 130 cm.
Robert J. Edwards Fund, Fanny P. Mason Fund and Arthur Gordon Tompkins Residuary
Fund. 64.709

One of a series of oils inspired by Les Sabines *by Jacques Louis David in the Louvre,
this is the second of the two Picassos to be acquired by the museum. Purchased the year
after it was painted, it brings to the collection a monumental late work that dramati-
cally illustrates Picasso's hatred of war, first expressed in his* Guernica *of 1937; the work
also synthesizes many of the artist's major forms of expression.*

References: Michel Leiris, *Picasso-Peintures, 1962–63* (Paris, 1964), p. 6, 7, no. 17; Christian
Zervos, *Pablo Picasso* (Paris, 1971), vol. 23, 121; Perry T. Rathbone in *Museum of Fine Arts, Boston:
Western Art* (Boston, 1971), no. 127.

128

Joan Miró, Spanish, born 1893
A toute épreuve
Book by Paul Eluard, published by Gérald Cramer, Geneva, 1958, illustrated with
woodcuts printed in color; 32 × 24.8 cm.
Seth K. Sweetser Fund. 58.573

*Great printmakers from Dürer to Picasso have frequently turned to book illustration.
In the museum's collection of rare books there are some extremely fine examples
ranging from the fifteenth century to the present. In the part of the collection representing the twentieth century no book is more exuberantly and joyfully illustrated than
Miró's* A toute épreuve.

References: James Thrall Soby, *Joan Miró* (New York, 1959), pp. 135–139, no. 29; Museum of
Fine Arts, Boston, and Harvard College Library, Department of Printing and Graphic Arts, *The
Artist and the Book, 1860–1960* (Boston, 1961), no. 209.

129

Nicholas de Staël, French (born in Russia), 1914–1955
Rue Gauguet
1949; oil on plywood panel; 200×240 cm.
Arthur Gordon Tompkins Residuary Fund. 57.385

Rue Gauguet *is one of the most heroic of de Staël's large pictures, built up entirely with a palette knife over a period of two years in de Staël's studio in the Rue Gauguet in Paris. "When nature is not the starting point," said de Staël, "the picture is inevitably bad." This belief is expressed in all his paintings, which reveal also the order and subtle color relationships he imposed.*

Reference: Roger v. Gindertael, "Nicolas de Staël," 1951, pl. 14; Museum of Fine Arts, Boston, *De Staël* (Boston, 1965), no. 20.

130

BERTO LARDERA, Italian, born 1911
Abstract Composition
1960; painted sheet iron; h. 1.3 m., w. 76.8 cm., d. 1.43 m.
Gift of Mrs. Peggy Guggenheim. 64.2200

The tremendous power of Lardera's Abstract Composition *depends upon the nature of his chosen material and its surface treatment, the intentional roughness of torch-cut edges, the interplay of jagged form and void, and the brute fashion in which the forms lunge out to organize the space around the piece. The combination of all of these factors gives to the work a dimension that exceeds its physical limits.*

Reference: Conil-Lacoste, "Lardera, découpeur d'espace," *L'Œil* (1958).

VI AMERICAN ART 17TH-20TH CENTURIES

131

Attributed to the FREAKE LIMNER
Robert Gibbs, 1665–1702
1670; oil on canvas; inscribed "AE·4¹/₂·A°·1670"; 101.6 × 83.8 cm
M. and M. Karolik Fund. 69.1227

The sole example of seventeenth-century American painting in the museum's collection, Robert Gibbs forms a group with portraits of his brother and sister, Henry and Margaret, owned by Mrs. David M. Giltinan, Sr. of West Virginia. The three are attributed to the Freake Limner, so named because of his portraits of John Freake and his wife and child in the Worcester Art Museum. The emphasis on two-dimensionality, linear ornamentation, and decorative use of color suggests that the Limner's inspiration derived from sixteenth-century Elizabethan painting. The portrait of Robert remained in the possession of the descendants of the sitter until its purchase by the museum.

References: Alan Burroughs, *Limners and Likenesses* (Cambridge, Mass., 1936), p. 42, no. 17; *American Paintings in the Museum of Fine Arts, Boston* (Boston, 1969), no. 1, fig. 1; *Centennial Acquisitions*, special issue of *Boston Museum Bulletin* 68 (1970), 106, no. 72.

132

Jeremiah Dummer, Boston, 1645–1718

Spout cup

Ca. 1680; silver; h. 12.4 cm., diam. of base 5.8 cm., diam. of lip 7.8 cm.

Gift of Mrs. Eugene G. Eppinger in memory of Stephen H. R. and Mary J. Codman. 63.273

The spout cup, used to feed small children and invalids, was a short-lived form made principally in New England in the late seventeenth and early eighteenth centuries. This is one of only two known spout cups by Dummer, both now in the museum's collection.

References: V. Isabell Mille, "American Silver Spout Cups," *Antiques* 44 (1943), 74, fig. 3; Kathryn C. Buhler, *American Silver, 1655–1825, in the Museum of Fine Arts, Boston* (Boston, forthcoming).

133

Teakettle

Probably New York ca. 1720; silver; h. 24.1 cm. with handle, diam. of body 16.5 cm.
Gift of Mrs. H. M. Goodwin. 64.18

The kettle bears no mark, but its style and generous size strongly suggest that it was made in New York. Once owned by a Hudson River Valley family, the kettle has a distinctive spout, and perhaps one day a marked kettle with spout cast from the same mold will be found to identify the unknown maker.

References: Alice Winchester, "Colonial Silversmith," *Antiques* 70 (1956); Museum of Fine Arts, Boston, *Colonial Silversmiths: Masters & Apprentices* (Boston, 1956); Kathryn C. Buhler, *American Silver, 1655–1825, in the Museum of Fine Arts, Boston* (Boston, forthcoming).

158

134

JACOB HURD, Boston, 1702–1758
Teakettle on stand
1730–1740; silver; h. 36.5 cm., diam. 19 cm.
Gift of Esther Lowell Abbot in memory of her mother, Esther Lowell Cunningham,
granddaughter of James Russell Lowell. 1971.347 a, b

*Made by one of the foremost Boston silversmiths, this is the only published New Eng-
land teakettle from the Colonial period. Originally owned by the Reverend John Lowell
(1704–1767), it has always belonged to members of the Lowell family and is engraved
with their coat of arms.*

Reference: Kathryn C. Buhler, *American Silver, 1655–1825, in the Museum of Fine Arts, Boston*
(Boston, forthcoming).

135

ZACHARIAH BRIGDEN, Boston, 1734–1787

Teapot

1760; silver; h. 15.2 cm., diam. of foot 7 cm.

Theodora Wilbour Fund in memory of Charlotte Beebe Wilbour. 1971.50

"The. Gift. of. Col¹: Epes. Sergeant. to. his. daughter. Mary. 1760" is engraved beneath the impaled Sargent-Winthrop coat of arms. Catherine Winthrop, Mary's mother and Epes Sargent's (1690–1762) second wife, was the great-granddaughter of Governor Winthrop of Massachusetts. As well as the Paul Revere bookplate made for Epes Sargent, Jr., the museum's collection includes a coffee pot made by Revere in 1781 for Mary's brother, Paul Dudley Sargent.

References: Museum of Fine Arts, Boston, *Colonial Silversmiths: Masters & Apprentices* (Boston, 1956); Kathryn C. Buhler, *American Silver, 1655–1825, in the Museum of Fine Arts, Boston* (Boston, forthcoming).

136

Sidechair

Newport, Rhode Island, ca. 1760; mahogany; h. 97.8 cm., w. 58.4 cm., d. 52.1 cm.

The Edwin E. Jack Fund. 1971.280

The precise outline and harmonious proportions of this Newport chair distinguish it from any other in the museum's collection. It has descended in a family now living in Massachusetts, who trace it back to Joseph Vose (1738–1816), a brigadier general in Washington's main army.

160

137

JOHN SINGLETON COPLEY, American, 1738–1815
Corkscrew Hanging on a Nail
1766–74; oil on panel; 8.9×9.5 cm.
Bequest of Ogden Codman. 1970.223

This little picture was painted on the library door of the Russell-Codman house in Lincoln, Massachusetts, where it remained until stored in the cellar at the time the library woodwork was replaced in the 1870's. A former owner of the house had the painting cut out of its old door and preserved in the house prior to its coming to the museum. Copley is said to have painted this corkscrew on an occasion when his host could not find one. "Allow me Sir," said Copley, "to see to it that your house is never again without a corkscrew." Not only is this the first American trompe l'oeil, it is also the earliest known American still life.

References: Perry T. Rathbone, "Rediscovery: Copley's Corkscrew," *Art in America*, 1965, pp. 48–51, no. 3; *American Paintings in the Museum of Fine Arts, Boston* (Boston, 1969), no. 269, fig. 54.

138

PAUL REVERE, Boston, 1735–1818
Copper plate for Epes Sargent
1764; copper; h. 8.9 cm., w. 7 cm.
Annie A. Hawley Bequest Fund. 59.517

Made for Colonel Epes Sargent, Jr. (1721–1779), a merchant of Gloucester, Massachusetts, this copper plate is engraved with the Sargent arms: argent a chevron between three dolphins embowed sable; crest a dolphin of the field. It is charged in Revere's account book under the date of September 27, 1764:

> Mr. Epes Sargent Junr D^r
> To Engraving your Arms on a Copper Plate   0–12–0
> to 150 Prints at 4/p^r Hun^d 0– 6–0

The Sargent arms are said to have been first used in this country by William Sargent, who lived in Charlestown in 1639 and was the grandson of Hugh Sargent of Courteenhall, Northampton, England.

139

JOHN SHAW, Annapolis, Maryland, 1745–1829

Speaker's desk

Ca. 1797; mahogany veneer on pine, satinwood inlay; h. 83.2 cm., w. 92.1 cm., d. 58.4 cm.

Gift of Mr. and Mrs. Robert B. Choate. 63.12

John Shaw came to Annapolis about 1773, when the city was the center of cultural as well as economic activity in Maryland. His patrons included not only the wealthy Maryland gentry but the state of Maryland as well. Shaw's advertisements in the Maryland Gazette indicate that his shop produced a wide variety of fine mahogany furniture, generally in the transitional Chippendale or Hepplewhite styles. He favored simple, elegant proportions in design and inlay for decorative effect. His work for the state included furniture for various public buildings in Annapolis, and his bill for furnishing the Senate Chamber of the State House is among those still extant. Many of the original furnishings for this room, including the Speaker's desk, which now stands on its dais in the center of the room, were reunited when the room was restored. The Senate desk bears Shaw's label and is nearly identical in design and decoration to this desk at the Boston Museum. Both desks are inlaid with the eagle of the Great Seal and satinwood bandings, and both have histories of ownership through Annapolis descendants.

References: "Some Recent Accessions," Museum of Fine Arts, Boston, *Bulletin* 61 (1963), 115; Richard H. Randall, Jr., *American Furniture* (Boston, 1965), pp. 76–79.

140

Attributed to SAMUEL McINTIRE, Salem,
Massachusetts, 1757–1811
Carved medallion and urn on perspective machine
1800–1810; pine; h. 91.8 cm., w. 60.6 cm.,
d. 46.4 cm.
Acquired by exchange. 60.532

*Viewing pictures in a perspective machine was
apparently a fashionable pastime in Salem around
1800. Two of these are listed in the estate inventory of one of the city's most prominent citizens,
Elias Hasket Derby. Inside the base of the machine,
colored and reversed prints are placed on a sliding
rack, which is tilted to catch the light, and the
viewer looks in the window behind the portrait
medallion. The carving of the medallion is
closely related to documented carvings by Salem's
celebrated architect and carver Samuel McIntire,
and the portrait is traditionally said to represent
the artist himself.*

Reference: Richard H. Randall, Jr., *American Furniture* (Boston, 1965), pp. 260–61.

164

141
Attributed to DUNCAN PHYFE, New York, 1768–1854
Card table
1810–1820; mahogany, crotch mahogany veneer; h. 74.9 cm., w. 91.4 cm., d. 48.3 cm.
Francis Bartlett Fund. 58.19

The very impressive supporting eagle, carved in three parts, was a favorite motif for carvers of the period. A similar table, with the eagle facing the other way, is in the Garvan Collection at Yale University.

A cabinetmaker of great skill and creative ability, a diligent worker and shrewd businessman, Duncan Phyfe opened his New York shop in 1792. Early productions were in the Sheraton style, but Phyfe's Empire furniture was so popular that his name has practically come to stand for that style in American furniture.

Reference: Richard H. Randall, "Sources of the Empire Style," *Antiques,* April, 1963, 452–453, fig. 3; Richard H. Randall, Jr., *American Furniture* (Boston, 1965), p. 137.

165

142
Attributed to CHARLES-HONORÉ LANNUIER, New York, 1779–1819
Sofa table
Ca. 1815; rosewood with mahogany, brass string inlay, painted and gilded; h. (on casters) 74 cm., l. (with drop leaves extended) 1.625 m., d. 71.5 cm.
Decorative Arts Special Fund. 65.1684

Created in the French mode, this extraordinary sofa table is a type rare in American furniture and produced chiefly in New York. It is attributed to Charles-Honoré Lannuier, a French ébeniste who came to New York City in the early nineteenth century and helped to popularize the French taste in America. Lannuier's highly skilled craftsmanship was influenced by Directoire, Consulat, and early Empire styles. The 1802 edition of La Mésangère's Les Meubles et Objets de Goût *illustrated many of the decorative elements favored by Lannuier: gilded central figural supports, the hocked animal foot, and ormolu design motifs.*

The elegant ormolu mounts and finely cut and fitted rosewood veneers of this table relate it to a similar sofa table attributed to Lannuier in the White House collection and to other known pieces of furniture bearing the Lannuier label or stamp.

References: The Newark Museum, *Classical America, 1815–1845* (Newark, N. J., 1963), p. 75, no. 13; Joseph T. Butler, *American Antiques 1800–1900: A Collector's History and Guide* (New York, 1965), pp. 37–38, no. 5.

166

143

ALBERT VAN BEEST, American, 1820–1860
New Bedford from Fairhaven
Ca. 1848; pen and brown ink, brown and gray wash, 32 × 72 cm.
M. and M. Karolik Collection. 55.709

*To study American drawing in its most prolific century, the nineteenth, one must know
the M. and M. Karolik Collection. Formed by Maxim Karolik and Henry P. Rossiter,
Curator of Prints and Drawings, over a fifteen-year period, some 1500 of the nearly
3000 pictures have been published in a two-volume catalogue. Although works by folk
artists were known through catalogues such as that of the Abby Aldrich Rockefeller
Collection, drawings by more sophisticated academic artists were not as well known.
When they were exhibited in 1962, the academic drawings were to many a veritable eye-
opener in the history of American art.*

*Typical of many nineteenth-century Americans, the marine painter Van Beest was
European (Dutch) born and trained. He emigrated to America, where he had a studio
in New York, but he is known best for his views of New Bedford, Massachusetts.*

Reference: **Museum of Fine Arts, Boston,** *M. and M. Karolik Collection of American Water
Colors and Drawings, 1800–1875* (Boston, 1962), no. 686.

144

Anonymous folk artist, American, nineteenth century
Family Group
Ca. 1840; watercolor on paper; 26.8 × 43.2 cm.
M. and M. Karolik Collection. 55.692

This sedate family portrait exhibits many of the delightful characteristics of folk pictures. In spite of the artist's shortcomings in representing volume and space, one can only admire the acute observation of facial characteristics that can differentiate between the two boys, who seem to be identical twins.

Reference: Museum of Fine Arts, Boston, M. and M. Karolik Collection of American Water *Colors and Drawings, 1800–1875* (Boston, 1962), no. 1056.

145
ANONYMOUS PHOTOGRAPHER, American, mid–nineteenth century
Group portrait
Daguerreotype; image: 25 × 30 cm.
Gift of Mrs. M. Graham Murdock. 1970.330

*This superbly preserved daguerreotype group portrait, still in its original frame, rivals
the finest painted group portraits of mid-nineteenth-century America in its dignity and
penetration of individual character. The gentleman seated second from the right is
believed to be President Franklin Pierce. The silvered metal daguerreotype plate on
which the image was captured is larger than the standard manufactured size. Such plates
of exceptional size, made to order, were referred to as "mammoth" plates.*

Reference: Beaumont Newhall, *The Daguerreotype in America,* rev. ed. (New York, 1968).

146

Georgе Caleb Bingham, American, 1811–1879
The Squatters
1850; oil on canvas; 63.5 × 76.2 cm.
Bequest of Henry L. Shattuck in memory of the late Ralph W. Gray. 1971.154

Once entitled Early Settlers, *this is one of two paintings by Bingham in the collection. Bingham's sketchbook includes drawings for both the old man and the young man in this painting, nos. 96, 44, now in the St. Louis Mercantile Library.*

Reference: American Paintings in the Museum of Fine Arts, Boston (Boston, 1969), no. 131, fig. 285.

147

FITZ HUGH LANE, American, 1804–1865
Boston Harbor
1850–1855; oil on canvas; 66.8 × 106.7 cm.
M. and M. Karolik Collection by exchange and gift of John Wilmerding. 66.399

An almost complete realist in his painting of nature, Lane is intensely aware of the subtleties of light and atmosphere. This dedication to realism provides us with an accurate historical topographical view of New England and, in this case, of Boston Harbor. Lane did several paintings of Boston Harbor, two of which are noted in Wilmerding, Fitz Hugh Lane *(Salem, Mass., 1964, nos. 20, 21).*

Reference: American Paintings in the Museum of Fine Arts, Boston *(Boston, 1969), no. 712, fig. 263.*

171

148

John La Farge, American, 1835–1910
The Fish
Ca. 1875–80; stained glass, leaded roundel set in square frame; h. (without frame)
67.3 cm., d. 6.3 cm.
Anonymous gift and Edwin E. Jack Fund. 69.1224

John La Farge's great gifts as a colorist found remarkable expression in stained glass. A true innovator in this ancient craft, La Farge was the inventor of opaline glass, which he used in hundreds of windows for private and public buildings. Perhaps his most celebrated major undertaking was the collaboration with architect H. H. Richardson on Boston's Trinity Church, for which he designed stained glass windows and murals.

172

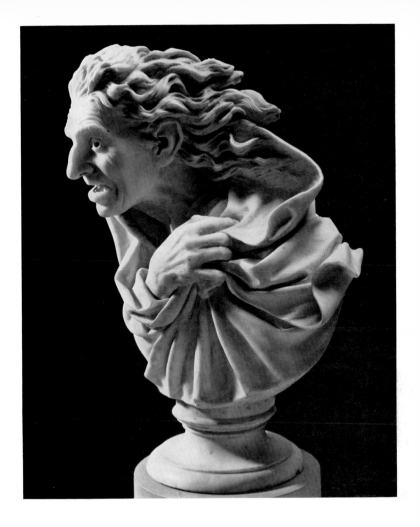

149

EDWARD R. THAXTER, Boston, 1854–1881
The Fury
Naples, 1881; marble; h. 66.1 cm.
William E. Nickerson Fund No. 2. 63.5

*Little is known of this New England sculptor. Possibly he was the son of the poetess
Celia Leighton, who married Levi Lincoln Thaxter, her teacher, at the lighthouse of
Shoals Island, Maine, in 1851. Thaxter may have received his training in Boston under
William Rimmer (1916–1879) and thereafter traveled to Florence in 1878. In 1881, at the
age of 27, he died of brain fever in Naples.*

*This emotionally expressive face, carved with intense realism, is signed "E. R. Thaxter."
In a period when aesthetic conventions were strongly directed against the baroque, it is
remarkable that Thaxter achieved such dramatic modeling of form. His work reveals a
deep understanding for Bernini and other related Neapolitan sculptors and shows
affinity to the naturalistic carvings of nineteenth-century Italian sepulchral sculpture.*

150

WINSLOW HOMER, American, 1836–1910

Clamming

1887; watercolor, sheet: 39.0 × 54.5; sight: 28.1 × 51.5 cm.; signed lower left in brush and black and gray wash: "Winslow Homer, 87"

Gift of John S. Ames. 65.1713

Winslow Homer, perhaps the greatest American watercolorist, is represented in the museum by over forty watercolors. Clamming *is a fine example of his work, but it is particularly interesting because of its drastic change in format that demonstrates Homer's creative process. He crossed out a foreground portion of water in front of the sandbar, so that the figure now takes on added weight and significance and is more firmly placed in the sand. The breadth of the elongated, horizontal composition augments the sense of calm and isolation of the mud flats at Prout's Neck, Maine.*

Reference: Museum of Fine Arts, Boston, *Winslow Homer* (Boston, 1959), no. 112.

151

CHARLES BURCHFIELD, American, 1893–1967

Spring Patterns

1917; watercolor; 45.5 × 54.2 cm.; signed lower right in pencil: "C. Burchfield 1917"

Sophie Friedman Fund. 1971.8

Charles Burchfield's involvement with nature and its forces was an intensely romantic one. In Spring Patterns, *one of four watercolors from the period 1915–1917 owned by the museum, Burchfield has penetrated and made visible the underlying design of rippling, reflecting water. The result is evocative of a certain light and atmosphere and is extraordinarily decorative.*

175

152

MAURICE B. PRENDERGAST, American, 1859–1924
Eight Bathers
1916–1918; oil on canvas; 71.8 × 61 cm.
Abraham Schuman Fund. 61.663

A late oil by this most innovative of the Eight and devotee of Cézanne, the Eight Bathers *is typical of Prendergast's characteristic use of oil on rough canvas. This picture is the result of reworking on earlier watercolor.*

Reference: Hedley Howell Rhys, *Maurice Prendergast, 1859–1924, [at the] Museum of Fine Arts, Boston* (Cambridge, Mass., 1960), p. 14.

153

CHARLES PRENDERGAST, American, 1863–1948

Carved and decorated chest

1926–27; wood and gessoed wood, carved, painted and gilded; h. 49.8 cm., l. 1 m. 28.9 cm., d. 48.9 cm.

Bequest of Mrs. Alice Wilder Smith. 67.732

A characteristic document of Charles Prendergast's mature period, this richly carved chest is one of only three ever made by this artist. Charles Prendergast began his career as a designer and maker of picture frames. He was nearly fifty when he made his first incised gesso panel. In this difficult and limited medium he created a unique and richly decorative style, combining gold, color, and linear rhythms. His art was influenced by that of his more famous brother, the painter Maurice Prendergast, by Persian miniatures, and by other Oriental, Near Eastern, Egyptian, Byzantine, and early Italian traditions. Yet his artistic vision is a highly personal one.

Reference: Richard J. Wattenmaker, *The Art of Charles Prendergast* (Boston, 1968).

154

LYONEL FEININGER, American, 1871–1956
Regler Church, Erfurt
1930; oil on canvas; 127 × 102 cm.
Charles Henry Hayden Fund. 57.198

Painted at Dessau, second home of the Bauhaus, Regler Church *is the largest of three paintings of similar composition that Feininger did of Erfurt, a town admired by the Bauhaus group for its numerous medieval churches. The picture clearly reflects both elements of French cubism and Feininger's interest in light and geometric construction.*

Reference: James W. Lane, "Feininger's Counterpoint in Paint: Lyonel out of Johann Sebastian," *Art News* 40 (March 1941), 38–39.

155

ALEXANDER CALDER, American, born 1898
Diana
Ca. 1934; walnut; h. 76.8 cm.
Decorative Arts Special Fund. 60.956

Calder's free spirit and limitless imagination led him to compose four jointed and movable pieces of wood (one of them actually a wooden cooking spoon) to suggest Diana the huntress with bow and shield, poised, alert, and ready for the hunt. This "mobile-stabile" is a fairly early demonstration of the artist's preoccupation with changing formal relationships. The subtle humor that characterizes the piece appears in much of Calder's work–the great circuses for example, and the twisted wire Cow, which is also in this museum's collection.

References: Hanns Swarzenski, "Recent Acquisitions of Contemporary Sculpture," Museum of Fine Arts, Boston, *Bulletin* 61 (1963), frontispiece, 99; Wallraf-Richartz Museum, Cologne, *Traum – Zeichen – Raum* (Cologne, 1965), no. 106.

156

JACKSON POLLOCK, American, 1912–1956
Number 10
1949; oil and aluminium paint on canvas; 45.7 × 271.7 cm.
Arthur C. Thompkins Fund and Sophie M. Friedman Fund. 1971.638

The first purchase of the new Department of Contemporary Art and the cornerstone of the contemporary collection, Number 10 was executed at the height of Pollock's career. The importance of his works, especially those from his classical "drip period" lies in the manner of paint application and overall fieldlike effects. The painting shows an inter-woven network of black pigment, light and atmospheric qualities of aluminum paint, and splashes of color. Despite the facture, the picture avoids disorder and mechanical rhythms. Charged with vitality from edge to edge, the painting has exceptional clarity and variety of accent.

References: Michael Fried, "Jackson Pollock," *Artforum* 4 (September 1965), 14–17; Frances V. O'Connor, *Jackson Pollock* (New York, 1967); William Rubin, "Jackson Pollock and the Modern Tradition," *Artforum*, February 1967, 14–22.

157

GEORGE RICKEY, American, born 1907
Red Vine
1959–1961; polychromed stainless steel; marble
base; h. 70.2 cm., w. (at widest point) 49 cm.
Gift of Mr. and Mrs. Stephen A. Stone and Arthur
Mason Knapp Fund. 66.195

*Red Vine represents the exploration of new possi-
bilities in space sculpture and kinetic design.
Constructed in six separate movable parts and
composed of leaf clusters on tall steel stems, the
work has a lyrical quality and an affinity to nature. Each part, set in a state of delicate balance,
is sensitive to the slightest touch or current of air,
and the surprising effects of the movements that
result are exploited as an aesthetic component.*

*Reference: George Rickey: Kinetic Sculptures (Boston,
1964).*

181

158

LEE GATCH, American, born 1902
Gothic Night
1957; oil on canvas; 107.3 × 117.4 cm.
Charles Henry Hayden Fund. 57.666

Expressing a direct visual experience, Gatch wrote "In my youth I was a hunter and the night forest fascinated me, especially the great arches made by the trees against the brilliant November sky. This was the visual experience that was to find spiritual discipline many years later." Another picture of similar composition entitled Leda *is in a New York collection.*

References: Barbara Guest, "Avery and Gatch, Lonely Americans," *Art News* 59 (1960), 42–45; Perry T. Rathbone, *Lee Gatch* (New York, 1960), pp. 12–13, 19, 37.

159

WILLEM DE KOONING, American, born in the Netherlands, 1904
Untitled
1949; black enamel on paper; 55.6×75.9 cm.
Sophie M. Friedman Fund. 1970.12

Although at first glance seemingly abstract, the bulging, fleshy shapes and grinning, toothy mouth of De Kooning's untitled drawing remind us that the artist's work has generally taken the human figure as its point of departure. The drawing is equivalent in size, technique, and black and white palette to many of his paintings of this period. It is the first work by De Kooning to be acquired by the museum.

160

ROBERT RAUSCHENBERG, American, born 1925
License
1962; lithograph printed in brown, black, and gray; image: 99.5 × 71 cm.
Lee M. Friedman Fund. 67.22

License *is one of the first prints by one of the most influential figures in the nineteen-sixties revival of printmaking by leading American painters. Its purchase is part of a continuing program of acquiring significant contemporary prints.*

Reference: Edward A. Foster, *Robert Rauschenberg: Prints 1948–1970* (Minneapolis, 1970), no. 8.

161

MORRIS LOUIS, American, 1912–1962
Theta
1961; acrylic resin paint on canvas; 259.1 × 326.7 cm.
Anonymous gift. 67.623

Theta *was presented to the museum shortly after the important Morris Louis retrospective exhibition in 1967. It is one of the series of "unfurleds," which Louis himself considered to be his greatest accomplishment, and marks the culmination of his search for a format through which color could achieve new, expressive eloquence. In these works, thinned pigment was stained into raw canvas. An astonishing, expansive feeling results from the dynamic composition in which the center is emptied, and ribbons of intense color are moved to the margins of the picture.*

References: Clement Greenberg, "Louis and Noland," *Art International* 4 (May 1960), 26–29; Kenworth Moffett, "Morris Louis: Unfurleds and Omegas," *Artforum* 8 (April 1970), 44–47.; Michael Fried, *Morris Louis* (New York, 1971).

162

DAVID SMITH, American, 1906–1965
Cubi XVIII
1964; polished stainless steel; h. 274 cm., w. of base 53.3 cm., d. of base 50.8 cm.
Anonymous Centennial Gift. 68.280

This sculpture is one of a series of twenty-eight related works called Cubi *that was begun in 1963 and remained uncompleted at the time of Smith's death the following year. Structures composed of cubes and cylinders of burnished steel are counterbalanced in tangential relationship creating a feeling of expansion and extension into space. The calligraphic polish of the surfaces gives these works a quality of weightlessness and creates reflections that relate the sculptural form to the surrounding atmosphere.*

References: Cleve Gray, *David Smith by David Smith* (New York, 1968); Edward Fry, *David Smith* (New York, 1969); Rosalind Krauss, *Terminal Ironworks: The Sculpture of David Smith* (Cambridge, Mass., 1970).

186

VII LOANS FROM THE ST. LOUIS ART MUSEUM

In our time, and especially in our country, the museum director is expected to be many things to many people—a jack-of-all-arts, as it were, in this admittedly odd profession. The measure of the director's success in shouldering all his obligations is the general health of his institution and the reputation it enjoys.

Yet what led the museum director into this complex discipline in the first place is often disregarded. That power is, simply, his innate love and understanding of art, supported by knowledge and informed by experience. This motivating force does not forsake him. It leads him on, and it finds its highest expression in works of art themselves. Every museum director knows that his most formidable challenge is the betterment of the collections to which he is committed. He dedicates himself to their expansion and their refinement to the end that their content becomes more useful and more meaningful in serving the everlasting function of art, which is to nourish mankind with insight, knowledge, and delight. In pursuing this aim, the director deals with eternal values. He knows that the affairs of the day that tower before him will fade; the real and lasting concern is the acquisition of a masterpiece. Paul J. Sachs, the mentor of my generation, admonished his students that the museum director's name is written in sand. Yet that director has the satisfaction of committing himself to those things whose worth will last "so long as men can breathe, or eyes can see."

My experience as director of the St. Louis Art Museum (then known as the City Art Museum) for fifteen years has significance beyond its local connotation because it was characteristically American. Art without boundary is the province of most American museums, and in many cases their art-inspired directors do not enjoy a complement of curatorial expertise to guide them. The director is thus obliged to exercise his own artistic judgment in many directions. The situation has, to be sure, serious drawbacks. Yet there is a compensating factor. The challenge of acquisition, of personal commitment, brings the director to terms with artistic expression of virtually every age and kind. The experience, aside from expanding his knowledge, sharpens his perception, broadens his sympathies, deepens his understanding. Narrow interest ripens into universal appreciation for all art.

To select the works for this section of the exhibition was exceedingly difficult, indeed, soul-searching. First of all, the request had to be tempered by consideration for my fellow director in St. Louis, whose generosity is quite clearly demonstrated here. Secondly, in order io point out the divergence of objects that challenges the solo director, it was necessary to omit certain works with which I most warmly identified myself. Other objects could not be lent because of their condition or fragility: the Sumerian bearded bull's head, for example, perhaps the most important of its kind in our country; or the brilliant white Meissen statuette of Augustus the Strong on its original bronze base; or the great Rodin bronze of John the Baptist Preaching, *cast under the sculptor's personal supervision; the late Rembrandt; or the famous Holbein. But there is satisfaction, even if of a sentimental kind, that my former, much-loved museum would lend my first acquisition, Lyonel Feininger's* Glorious Victory of the Slopp "Maria," *and my last, the magnificent portrait of a woman by Frans Hals.*

Perry Townsend Rathbone

189

163

Hippopotamus

Egypt, Dynasty 12, 1991–1786 B.C.; faience; h. 9.5 cm., l. 18.7 cm.

Gift of Miss Martha Love, 1952. 242.52

Among the many kindred hippopotami, this example is especially distinguished for its subtle modeling and perfect integration of the lotus motif and the animal's anatomy.

Collection: Comtesse de Behague, Paris.

Reference: J. Capart, *Documents pour servir à l'étude de l'art égyptien* (Paris, 1931), vol. 2, pl. 45.

164

Ritual Vessel (Fang Lei)

Chinese, early Chou Dynasty, ca. 1027–900 B.C.; cast bronze; h. 62.7 cm., w. 37.8 cm.

Museum Purchase, 1941. 2.41

References: *Bulletin of the City Art Museum of St. Louis* 26 (1941), 41 ff.; J. Edward Kidder, Jr., *Early Chinese Bronzes in the City Art Museum of St. Louis* (St. Louis, 1956), p. 68, pl. XVIII.; Max Loehr, *Ritual Vessels of Bronze Age China* (Greenwich, Conn., 1968), no. 43.

190

165

Plate

Persia, Samarkand, 10th century; Afrasiab ware; h. 6.7 cm., d. 37.2 cm.

Museum Purchase, 1951. 283.51

The perfectly designed cufic inscription reads, "Deliberation before the work protects you from regret."

References: "Some Middle Eastern Ceramics in City Art Museum of St. Louis," *Oriental Art* 55 (1958), 116, fig. 2; Kurt Erdmann, "Eine neue Gattung persischer Keramik," *Pantheon* 18 (1960), 4; Charles K. Wilkinson, *Iranian Ceramics* (New York, 1963), 55, 122, no. 22.

166

Workshop of ROGER OF HELMARSHAUSEN, Hildesheim, ca. 1130

Corpus from a cross

Bronze; h. 17.8 cm.

Museum Purchase, 1949. 73.49

One of the leading goldsmiths of the twelfth century whose name we know, Roger was active chiefly in Helmarshausen and Lower Saxony.

Collection: Hohenzollern, Sigmaringen; Joseph Brummer, New York.

References: Museum of Fine Arts, Boston, *Arts of the Middle Ages, 1000–1400,* 1949 (Boston, 1940), no. 263; H. Stewart Leonard, in *Bulletin of the City Art Museum of St. Louis* 35 (1950), 8 fig. 5; Hanns Swarzenski, *Monuments of Romanesque Art* (Chicago, 1954), p. 57, fig. 239, pl. 105.

192

167

Orphrey from a chasuble
France, early 15th century; linen, silk and gold thread embroidery; h. 105.5 cm.,
w. 60.2 cm.
Museum Purchase, 1949. 76.49

This orphrey originally decorated an ecclesiastical vestment. The Crucifixion is represented with the sorrowing Virgin and St. John at the foot of the Cross. Delicately colored threads of silk delineate the figures, which stand out against the rich checkerboard background of metallic gold thread.

Reference: Museum of Fine Arts, Boston, *Arts of the Middle Ages* (Boston, 1940), no. 108, pl. 61.

168

Aquamanile

Flemish, ca. 1450; bronze (latten); h. 41 cm.

Museum Purchase, 1949. 55.49

This aquamanile is fashioned in the shape of a medieval tower symbolizing the incarceration of St. Barbara, whose image appears on the front. Projecting from the base, a spigot terminates in a grotesque animal head. The aquamanile rests on three straight legs with feet in the form of long, pointed shoes, known as sollerets.

Collection: Baron de Decker, Brussels; Joseph Brummer, New York.

Reference: Museum of Fine Arts, Boston, *Arts of the Middle Ages, 1000–1400* (Boston, 1940), no. 294.

169

GIOVANNI MARIA, Castel Durante, active 1510–1520
Plate
Lustred majolica; h. 4.1 cm., diam. 22.8 cm.
Museum Purchase, 1942. 72.42

The work of this artist, one of the greatest Renaissance potter-painters, is characterized
by the highly personal use of classical motifs, scrolls, masks, and cupids.

Collection: Baron Gustave de Rothschild, Paris.
Reference: Bernard Rackham, *Guide to Italian Majolica* (London, 1933), pp. 54 f.

170

GIOVANNI DA BOLOGNA, Florentine (born Flemish), 1524–1608
The Bird Catcher
Late 16th century; gilt bronze; h. 30.6 cm.
Museum Purchase, 1951. 284.51

Other casts are in the Museo Nazionale, Florence; Castello Sforzesco, Milan; and
Staatliche Museen, Berlin.

Collections: Miller von Aichholz, Vienna; Alexander C. De Frey.
Reference: Wilhelm von Bode, *Italienische Bildwerke der Renaissance* (Berlin, 1930), vol. 2,
p. 36, no. 167, pl. 56.

171

FRANS HALS, Dutch, 1580/85–1666
Portrait of a woman
Ca. 1650–55; oil on canvas; h. 102.5 cm., w. 89.0 cm.
Art Museum Special Fund, Friends of the Art Museum, Donors, 1955. 272.55

*Hals' genius for a balanced expression of dignified reserve and natural ease is brilliantly
expressed in this lustrous late work from his so-called black period.*

Collection: Robert Sterling Clark, Williamstown, Massachusetts.
References: C. Hofstede de Groot, *A Catalogue Raisonné of the Works of the Most Eminent
Dutch Painters of the Seventeenth Century* (London, 1910), vol. 3, pl. 114, no. 396; W. R. Valentiner, *Frans Hals Paintings in America* (Westport, 1936), p. 95; Seymour Slive, *Frans Hals* (London,
1970), vol. 1, p. 184.

172

LODEWICK SUSI, Flemish-Italian, mentioned 1616–1620
Still Life
Signed and dated, 1619; oil on mahogany panel; h. 35 cm., w. 46.5 cm.
Museum Purchase, 1949. 50.49

This is one of the few known works of Susi, who introduced Flemish concepts of still life painting into Italy.

References: C. Sterling, *La Nature morte de l'antiquité à nos jours* (Paris, 1952), p. 58, pl. 22; *Das italienische Stilleben* (Zurich, 1964–1965), p. 34.

173

JOHN GREENWOOD, American, 1727–1792
Sea Captains Carousing in Surinam
Ca. 1758; oil on bed ticking; h. 95.8 cm., w. 191 cm.
Museum Purchase, 1948. 256.48

Surinam, or Dutch Guiana, was a favorite colony with American sea captains engaged in trade. Many of the seafarers seen here, natives of Newport and Providence, later became distinguished citizens occupying high offices in the Colonies. Among those identified are Captain Nicholas Cooke, later governor of Rhode Island; Captain Esek Hopkins, later first Commander in Chief of the Continental Navy, and his brother Stephen Hopkins, later a signer of the Declaration of Independence; also Jonas Wanton, Ambrose Page, Godfrey Malbone of Newport, and the artist. This painting, probably influenced by a print by Hogarth, is the earliest genre work by an American artist. Greenwood, active in his native Boston as a portrait artist until his sojourn in Surinam, later became a leading auctioneer in London.

References: A. L. A. Portrait Index (1906), 715; "John Greenwood, The Man and his Work," Bulletin of New York Public Library 31 (August 1927), 8; Alan Burroughs, John Greenwood in America (Andover, 1943), pp. 45, 47, 71; fig. 37.

198

174

GEORGE CALEB BINGHAM, American, 1811–1879
The Wood Boat
1850; oil on canvas; h. 62.8 cm., w. 75.3 cm.
Museum Purchase, 1951. 15.51

A drawing for the boy, the standing man, and the seated man at the right are in the Bingham sketch book in the Mercantile Library, St. Louis, pp. 94, 101, and 51, respectively. The reproduction of Bingham's preparatory drawing for the central figure in a Life *magazine article led to the discovery of this once lost painting in the attic of a Pittsburgh house. The article featured the St. Louis Museum exhibition "Mississippi Panorama" in 1949.*

References: F. Rusk, *George Caleb Bingham* (Jefferson City, 1917), pp. 51, 122; E. Maurice Bloch, *George Caleb Bingham* (Berkeley, 1967), pp. 104–105, 108–110, pl. 66; idem, *George Caleb Bingham: A Catalogue Raisonné* (Berkeley, 1967), no. 191, pp. 74–75.

175

Winslow Homer, American, 1836–1910
The Country School
1871; oil on canvas; h. 54.3 cm., w. 97.5 cm.
Museum Purchase, 1946. 123.46

That once familiar American institution, the one-room school house, is here immortalized in one of Winslow Homer's most enchanting early works. Two oil studies for the work are known, one in the Addison Gallery, Andover, the other in the Edwin D. Hewitt collection, New York.

References: W. H. Downes, *Homer* (Boston, 1911), p. 70; L. Goodrich, *Winslow Homer* (New York, 1944), pl. 9; Perry T. Rathbone, in *Bulletin of the City Art Museum of St. Louis* 32 (1947), 95 ff.; A. Ten Eyck Gardner, *Winslow Homer, American Artist: His World and His Work* (New York, 1961), pp. 238, 246; pl. on p. 36.

176

EDVARD MUNCH, Norwegian, 1863–1944
Moonlight
1896; color woodcut; h. 40.2 cm., w. 47.2 cm.
Gift of Gen. and Mrs. Leif. J. Sverdrup, 1952. 338.52

Reference: G. Schiefler, *Verzeichnis des graphischen Werks Edvard Munchs bis 1906* (Berlin, 1907), no. 81 B.

177 *(see overleaf)*

LYONEL FEININGER, American, 1871–1956
The Glorious Victory of the Sloop "Maria"
1926; oil on canvas; h. 54.6 cm., w. 85.1 cm.
Museum Purchase, 1940. 848.40

The Los Angeles County Museum has the watercolor dated 26.8.25.

The dichotomy of Feininger's life, half American, half German, is nicely reflected in this brilliant work, for, though painted in Germany, it celebrates a famous nineteenth-century victory in the America's Cup races off Newport, Rhode Island.

Collection: Staatsgalerie, Dresden.

References: Perry T. Rathbone, in *Bulletin of the City Art Museum of St. Louis* 25 (1940) 53–54; Robert Rosenblum, *Cubism and Twentieth Century Art*, p. 205, fig. 143; San Francisco Museum of Art, *Lyonel Feininger Memorial Circulating Exhibition* (1959), no. 33; H. Hess, *Lyonel Feininger* (New York, 1961), no. 265, pp. 108 f., 273.

178
DAVID SMITH, American, 1906–1965
Cockfight
1945; steel; h. 114.5 cm.
Museum Purchase, 1946. 188.46

Probably the first work by David Smith to be acquired by any museum, this early sculpture already displays this artist's extraordinary originality and independence in both form and technique.

Reference: Fogg Art Museum, Harvard University, *David Smith, 1906–1965: A Retrospective Exhibition* (1966), p. 69.

202